A STUDY OF HEBREW THOUGHT

A Study of

Hebrew Thought

by

CLAUDE TRESMONTANT

translated by

MICHAEL FRANCIS GIBSON

DESCLEE COMPANY

NEW YORK - TOURNAI - PARIS - ROME   1960

NIHIL OBSTAT

MYLES M. BOURKE, S.T.D., S.S.L.

Censor Librorum

IMPRIMATUR

✠ FRANCIS CARDINAL SPELLMAN

ARCHBISHOP OF NEW YORK

November 16, 1959

The nihil obstat and imprimatur are official declarations that a book or pamphlet is free of doctrinal or moral error. No implication is contained therein that those who have granted the nihil obstat and imprimatur agree with the contents, opinions or statements expressed.

LIBRARY OF CONGRESS CATALOG CARD NUMBER 60-6516

This is a translation from ESSAI SUR LA PENSÉE HÉBRAÏQUE (2nd Edition, 1956, Les Éditions du Cerf, Paris).

Printed in Belgium

Ἡ ΚΑΘ' ΕΒΡΑΙΟΥΣ ΦΙΛΟΣΟΦΙΑ

Clement of Alexandria

TABLE OF CONTENTS

Adequatio rei et intellectus, the equation of reality and mind—this is how the medieval philosophers see the nature of truth, *veritas*. According to this classical definition, truth is where there is harmony, where thing and thought agree. But much more is enshrined in the four Latin words. Things *are*, and are true, because they were first thought by God. His mind is the wellspring of their being, and in knowing them, we reflect some of His knowledge. The knower is also a "conqueror"; he makes things his own, yet his conquest of reality is a humble one, for he knows it truly only when he surrenders to it.

Although they go beyond it, these affirmations are rooted in the Greek philosophical tradition. Quite different is the biblical concept of truth, *emet*. Unconcerned with any theory of knowledge, the ancient Hebrews turned their attention to life, above all, to life in the presence of God. In the language of Scripture, true is what stands firm, what is stable, valid and binding, what endures and can be relied on.

Thus in a biblical context truth may mean steadfastness. "The God of truth" is the God who is ever faithful, true to His promise, the God under whose shield man is secure, the God who is refuge and fortress to those who obey His word. Again, truth may be a synonym of trustworthiness. About to choose helpers to whom he can delegate authority, Moses looks for men able, God-fearing, incorruptible, for "men of truth," that is, men upright and dependable (Ex. 18: 21). To serve God "in sincerity and truth" means to serve Him with undivided devotion and perfect fidelity (Jos. 24: 14). Finally, truth may stand for the divine teaching, the authentic doctrine, the true faith, the right way of life. Hence truth is not something merely to be thought about or spoken of, but something to be carried out. The man who shuns the company of the wicked "walks in God's truth" (Ps. 25: 3); fulfilling His will, he "does the truth" (Tob 4: 6; John 3: 21).

To the ancient Hebrews, then, truth is not an idea but a living thing. The very moment the children of Israel, fearing and trusting

God, attend to His demands, truth springs out of the earth (Ps. 84: 12). When they depart from the right way, truth stumbles in the market place, indeed vanishes and is missing from their midst (Is. 59: 14-15). With an idol enthroned in the Temple, with false worship supplanting the sacrifice to the living God, with power subverting the true faith, "truth is cast to the ground" (Dan. 8: 12). And in the fullness of time the unheard-of is heard: "I am the truth" (John 14: 6). In Christ God reveals Himself and addresses man, not in empty words but in words that are deeds and love; in Christ God's Word is made flesh and tents with us. Now the promise of promises is fulfilled. Salvation is come, truth lives among men.

Truth is not the only word with a special biblical significance. Other key words of Scripture, justice, peace, poverty among them, do not have the same meaning for a Roman or modern as for a Hebrew ear; their origin and home are in a world whose vision of man and of the creatures about him, of time and eternity, are often at variance with Western or, for that matter, Eastern views of the universe. In order to grasp the biblical message we must, at times, unlearn our own speech and learn another language, if not its every term, at least its spirit. For Holy Scripture is not the Word of God pure and simple—man could never hear it —but His Word channeled through the ancient Israel, preached by Hebrew men of old; His Word thought by Hebrew minds, even when their lips spoke and their hands wrote Greek.

No doubt, one can overstate the importance of Hebrew thought patterns; any man, whether he knows them or not, is loved by God and can love Him in return. Still, we dare not ignore the medium God adopted to disclose His will and saving design. For were we to take no note of the particularly Hebrew vision of earth, heaven, and man, we should never master the fullness of the biblical world nor enjoy all its wealth, we should not move in the land of our rebirth as freely as becomes citizens nor be at home in it as we are in our native land. *Sentire cum ecclesia*, to think and to be of one mind with the Church, this Catholic rule of life can well be said to include the admonition: *sentire cum scriptoribus sacris*, to think and to be of one mind with the sacred writers of Scripture.

It must have been reflections like these that prompted Claude Tresmontant to study the metaphysical structure of the Bible and compare it with the metaphysical approach of Greek and modern thinkers. Time and again, we have been told that prophecy is the special domain of the ancient Hebrews and philosophy that of the Greeks; we are, therefore, inclined to see in "biblical metaphysics" a contradiction in terms.   It is true, Hebrew prophecy is unique; the Israel of biblical times lacked the philosophical bent that marked Greek intellectual life and thus lacked great thinkers.   Hebrew thought is unspeculative.   Never pondering over propositions, never weighing arguments or evolving theories, it is always the profession of a faith that commits the whole man.   Still, it is not devoid of metaphysical foundations nor could it be, for no man, not even the primitive, can look at and interpret the world without some basic metaphysical concepts.

The great metaphysical truth with which Tresmontant begins his study is the one that opens the Bible: The visible world is *created*.   Compared with the Platonic view of the world, this is a revolutionary doctrine; seen against the background of the Meso-potamian myth on cosmic origins, with which the sacred writer of Genesis was undoubtedly acquainted, it is even more: a new and happy message, a gospel.   In the Mesopotamian myth the universe is the result of hatred and revenge, of a fierce war among the gods, plotting destruction against one another, of the slaying of the father and of the mother, "chaos," by their own children. In Genesis it is the work of a loving God who in His infinite goodness gives existence and life to His creatures, of a God who need not contend with other gods nor fight chaos, of a God who can say: "Be!" and things are.

A created universe is a meaningful universe.   No dungeon or dark cave, the world of senses is to the biblical man one of joy and wonder, resounding with words of its Maker.   Things seen are not mere shadows; even the things he touches, tastes, or smells, speak.   They speak of God, they speak to man, and man listens to them; therefore the Hebrew reverence for the sensible world. God is a consuming fire, a rock; like fragrant oil His spirit is poured out over all flesh; His voice roars like a lion's; His goodness can be tasted.   Israel is a vineyard, the just man a tree planted near streams of water, and his prayer rises like incense before the Lord. In this spiritual perception of the world of sight and touch and the other senses, in this predilection for the concrete, the Christian recognizes an incarnational outlook that finds its fulfillment in the supreme event of all time: God's coming in the flesh.

All the man of antiquity could see when reflecting on time was its transitory character.   Life was a race toward death.   Thus

Horace wrote: *Eheu fugaces... labuntur anni*, in Barham's translation, "Years glide away, and are lost to me, lost to me!" (*Odes*, II, 14). In the perspective of Scripture, however, time is growth, movement toward a goal. It is the meeting ground of God and man. In time the timeless God revealed Himself, speaking to Abraham, Moses, and the prophets, speaking in Jesus Christ. In time man works out his eternal salvation. Time, then, is a sacred trust; history has a sacramental quality, for in visible events the invisible God visits His people.

As part of the prodigious doctrine of creation, Claude Tresmontant discusses the dialectics of the one and the many: The multitude of creatures, which to the Greeks seemed a fall, was to the Hebrews an ascent. There are other basic concepts of biblical thinking the author examines: man, the union of soul and body; the pneumatic order; Israel, the people marked by the sign of the Exodus; the interdependence of mind and action, the knowledge of the heart. There are still others, but I shall be silent about them, for I do not wish to rob the reader of what awaits him: the discovery of a new world or rather of the timeliness of the ancient world of the Bible. I remember well the joy with which I read the *Essai sur la pensée hébraïque* when it first appeared in 1953.

Tresmontant has gathered a great deal of biblical material, and with a masterful hand made transparent its hidden metaphysical texture. With every page bespeaking his love for the Word of God and its human instrumentality, his study is a notable aid to a living and lived understanding of Holy Scripture. This is not to say that his presentation leaves no room for disagreement. I, for instance, think his rejection of "matter as the principle of individuation" hasty, because he ignores the distinction made by many Thomists between individuation and individuality or personhood. In relating the Marxist view of history as an inescapable march toward the liberation of the proletariat—a dialectical advance transcending the will of individuals—to the prophetic vision of history as the labor, the birthpangs, of a new world, Tresmontant seems again the victim of too quick a judgment. Momentarily, he forgets that the prophets championed the cause of the oppressed, not because they considered themselves the interpreters of a historical evolution but because they were the spokesmen of the Holy One of Israel, and that the goal toward which history strains is not the abolition of classes but the realization of God's undisputed kingship. Moreover, there is no unfailing progression that will establish

His rule, there is only the unfailing power of grace and the consent, the turning to Him, of individuals.

The author deserves our gratitude for denouncing any attempt to hypostasize matter, to bisect man, as if body and soul were two alien, not to say hostile, entities. But I do not think he is right when he suggests that, though St. Thomas generally upholds the indivisibility of the person, he and Aristotle lean at times towards a dichotomy of man. To speak only of Aristotle, in his *De Anima* the Philosopher holds it to be no less unsound to say that the soul is angry than to say that it weaves or builds houses; it is not the soul but the whole man who, thanks to his soul, thinks, learns, and takes pity. Aristotle even insists that since only a living being can be fed, it is not the body but the besouled body, *to empsychon sōma*, that takes food (408 b and 416 b). Tresmontant himself quotes similar texts. On this point, then, Aristotle's view is not very different from the biblical vision, which sees man as a being in whom the material and the spiritual interpenetrate one another. This vision, and no other, is the metaphysical foundation on which both the sacramental order and our hope of resurrection rest. For the recipient of divine grace is not a disembodied soul but the whole man, and because he is spirit in the flesh, spirit and flesh will share in eternal bliss.

Our debt to the unified world view of the Israel of old is unique and lasting. Yet, we would suffer a tremendous loss were we to disregard the contributions of the Greeks to our theological, philosophical, and scientific thinking, and not the least among their gifts are the art of distinction as well as the categories, so often today lightly dismissed. There can be no return for us to the undifferentiated world of the ancient Hebrews which, as Tresmontant points out, is the world of shepherds and farmers. There can be no return for us, because ours is, as a matter of fact, no longer the gloriously simple world of country folk but also because revealed truth draws into its orbit, as a matter of right, other worlds, other ways, other thought patterns. The Church, so the Fathers marvel, is heir to the "treasures of the Egyptians" (see Ex. 12: 36); as a living organism she must by her very nature assimilate whatever is true, good, and beautiful, even though it has grown in a garden of mere human planting. Tresmontant is quite explicit on this. There can, then, be no return for us to a world stripped of all we providentially acquired; what we need is reorientation. Our thought and life have been, and will continue to be, enriched by the *logoi spermatikoi,* the seeds of truth entrusted to the nations. But as we thus move forward, we must never cease to look back and hearken to the voice of the past: the religious experience of God's people and its expression, for He made them the vehicle by which to convey to all men the knowledge of His mysteries.

When, a moment ago, I drew attention to what I consider some minor flaws in the author's presentation, I did so for the sake of truth and not for the sake of criticism. In fact, I hope that the expression of a few disagreements, rather than sweeping praise, will convince the reader of my genuine admiration for Tresmontant's work. In a few instances, his language is not as precise as I should wish it to be, but to dwell on one or the other inexact word would be ungrateful. His book is the work of a pioneer—he himself calls it an *essai*—and as such it is a remarkable achievement. Its greatest merit, it seems to me, is to have given us a fresh perspective of the biblical teaching on creation. While the modern mood—I deliberately say "mood," and not "science"—in its *ressentiment* against anything not subject to man's command and in its neurotic bent toward a life of darkness, favors a universe emptied of meaning, the Bible proclaims a universe moved by love. Thus Dante can call God *lieto fattore,* the "joyous Maker" (*Purgatorio,* XVI, 89).

So basic is the doctrine of the Creator, majestic, sovereign, yet delighting in and blessing His work, that without this doctrine sin can be recognized but never its real horror: its offense against the holiness of God. Yet without true awareness of sin, the world will not repent, and without repentance there can be no forgiveness, without forgiveness no healing, no salvation, no hope. Tresmontant's book is an impressive reminder of the truth the Church has always lived by, that the divine Author of the Law, of the Prophets, and of the Writings of the Apostles is *one;* that the gospel of redemption completes and crowns the gospel of creation. Only among a people that believed in the lasting goodness of the Creator and the original goodness of man could Christ, the Restorer, have been born, have taught, have died and risen.

JOHN M. OESTERREICHER
The Institute of Judaeo-Christian Studies
Seton Hall University

Speaking as a layman I consider two aspects of this book important.

The first is that it makes a most significant distinction. Common opinion has too often confused Christianity with doctrines that are foreign to it. Not a few people seem to believe that it teaches what is in fact a form of Manichean dualism, condemning sensible reality and inviting us to turn from it to "matters of the soul." To assert this openly is a sign of monstrous ignorance, especially monstrous because of the far reaching consequences of such a doctrine. Yet even people too erudite to accept the terms of such a definition still subscribe to it unconsciously.

Of course the danger of this confusion is that Christianity is often rejected along with the errors it would be the first to condemn.

This is not so much a matter of theory as it is a matter of fact. Because of our education, and because of the philosophy that pervades the very air we breathe, we are formed in intellectual principles which, once blended with the Word of God, produce very strange results indeed.

This matter can only be unravelled historically, by tracing our unquestioned axioms to their several sources. Once this is done we may discover the true originality of Christian thought and realize how strange was the confusion of such essentially different systems. For while the Neo-Platonic doctrines, however noble, cut man from the world and close him within himself, Christian doctrine leads us to the world and, through the world, to God. The first is a movement inward, a natural asceticism that is bound to fail because of man's own finite nature; the second goes outward, it is a supernatural transformation that finds sustenance in the bounty of God. For while the first proposes that man should suffice himself and attain salvation by his own efforts, the second teaches us our fundamental insufficiency and that we should allow God to help us. "Strength is made perfect in weakness."

I believe this book discovers what sickness, what contamination have made God's truth appear inhuman and unreal. We may hope too that it will reconcile faith with fact in the reader's mind, by showing that faith leads to, and not away from what contemporary psychologists call reality.

This book is of contemporary interest for a second reason.   The metaphysics drawn from Hebrew Scriptures is founded on reality, a reality which the sciences: physics and astrophysics, biology and palaeontology, medicine and psychology, are making known to us.   Not in the outer form of the narrative but in the profound aspects of its metaphysics, the Bible's notion of creation and definition of time reappear in scientific theory, as does its representation of man in the findings of psychology.   Such a consideration should not move the scientific thinker as such, nor compel him to any conclusion; nor should it move the theologian as a theologian; but it should contribute to appeasing the apprehensions which sometimes move the spokesmen of belief to brand one science or another an intruder on the sacred grounds.   As they proceed with different methods (and with different objects) it seems good cause for mutual trust to see that the metaphysics of science and the metaphysics of Revelation find agreement in the deepest *matters.*

A word should be said about the translation of the biblical texts. I have done my best to preserve the literal sense of these texts without departing too far from the accepted English translations.

Also some small changes have been made, by the author, or with his approval.   Some passages have been deleted, and a paragraph inserted in part II on the biblical meaning of "Heart."

MICHAEL FRANCIS GIBSON

ACKNOWLEDGMENT

I wish to acknowledge my indebtedness and express my gratitude to Father John Courtney Murray s. j. who gave much of his valuable time to reviewing the manuscript of my translation. If any faults slipped through, they should be ascribed, not to an inadvertency on his part, but to a persistency in ignorance on my own.

M. F. G.

This work is a sketch, a blueprint.

We shall try to outline a manner of thought, to uncover the main lines, the organic structure of a metaphysics which is truly, though implicitly, contained in the Bible. It is on this metaphysics that revealed biblical theology rests. Above all we wish to show the deeper implications of this system which is the underlying prerequisite of Revelation.

To give this sketch some perspective we shall use comparison and contrast. The philosophy we wish to portray will be set beside the native tendencies of Greek philosophy, especially those tendencies which, throughout the history of thought, have proven incompatible with the metaphysics whose inspiration is biblical. Certain aspects of Platonism and, above all, of Neo-Platonism show themselves as the irreconcilable opponents of these systems. The fundamental outlook — be it conscious or not — the basic concepts, the premises and the problematics of these conflicting philosophies are so thoroughly different that no agreement between them could possibly be worked out. Quid ergo Athenis et Hierosolymis?

Our reader may wonder at the considerable attention given to the examination of Bergson's writings. Bergson's studies proved a great help to us in finding and defining the distinctive features of Hebrew metaphysics. The comparison also allowed us better to appreciate Bergson whose theses have too often remained unknown and neglected.

What is more, because this book took shape by confronting and opposing the metaphysics of the Bible and Neo-Platonism, we felt that it would be useful to stress how two very different currents meet and fuse in Bergson's mind. One is akin to Hebrew thought. It is that part of Bergson which conflicts with Greek philosophy: his criticism and psychoanalyses of the Ancients. The other, heir to Neo-Platonism, revives the postulates and aspirations of Plotinus.

In Chapter I, on Creation and Time, we draw upon Bergson in so far as he helps us clarify the metaphysical stand of the Bible. We have added an appendix to show what elements relate Bergson to Plato, Plotinus and Spinoza. It is because of these elements that Bergson's philosophy cannot be reconciled with the metaphysics we find in the Bible, nor with Christian philosophy.

The problem of Christian philosophy is never entirely out of sight. The reader will notice that the main points of biblical metaphysics foreshadow the "requirements of Christian philosophy" laid down by Aquinas, Blondel or Laberthonnière. The metaphysical construction implied by Revelation is essentially the same as that which is vital to any theology founded on the Bible.

We have limited ourselves to a study of the metaphysical positions that underly biblical theology. We have not taken up questions that concern biblical theology itself.

Still it is difficult, in the world of the Bible, to separate philosophy from theology. Here philosophy is not an end. It is not a separate system. Some points we touch upon are not strictly within its boundaries. Theology must claim the parts of our chapter on biblical anthropology that speak of a supernatural factor in man: *ruah*, the Spirit.

Now let us state our aims:

— to uncover the important features of the metaphysical system implicitly present in the Bible;

— to show in what way this system resembles and differs from the major trends of Greek philosophy;

— to contribute towards a definition of the requirements and essence of Christian philosophy;

— to define the permanent current of Gnostic philosophy in relation to Christian philosophy and establish its significance.

Finally, it seems that such an attempt to analyze and to discern the hidden tendencies and the inner orientation immanent in structures of thought ought to raise the question of initial options — those secret choices from which systems proceed — the discernment of spirits.

Part one

CREATION
AND THE
CREATED

chapter one

CREATION

This world, this sensible world is *created*. Such a proposition holds nothing startling for us. Yet to the several Greek metaphysics it came as a radically new pronouncement, a revolution; and such it remains to the modern philosophies which have retained the metaphysical principles of antiquity.

To Plato, the sensible world proceeds from the intelligible through "imitation" *(mimesis)*. The former is a shadow of the latter. In Platonism it is this "participation" which holds the place that "creation" holds in the Bible. True, creation does imply participation, but participation does not exhaust the implications of creation. Creation is much more than a participation.

Plotinus considers that the sensible and the multiple proceed from the One by a degradation, a fall, a scattering through time and space.

To Spinoza particular things are but "modes of the divine attributes." We may deduce them from the notion of God just as, from the notion of a triangle, we deduce that the sum of the angles is equal to two right angles.

Leibnitz regards the multiplicity of monads as but a multiplicity of viewpoints; a way by which the One increases through multiplication while never ceasing to be himself the One, *monas monadum*.

To Hegel, nature is an alienation of the Spirit. In this proposition we discover one of the themes of the Cabala, ＊ the theme of "exile"

＊ In the Cabala, contrary to biblical tradition, there is no creation; in this sense the metaphysics of Cabala is much closer to Neo-Platonism than it is to the Scriptures. "Fundamenta Philosophiae... quae omnem Creationem propie dictam negat, Essentiamque supponit Divinam quasi Corporeo-Spiritualem, Mundumque Materialem aliquo modo Spiritum." *Kabbala Denudata*, 1677, t. I, pars 2a, p. 293.

of the Shekhina, the theme of the "sparks emprisoned" within matter. This is a Gnostic theme, traces of which are found in Manichean doctrine.

In all of these philosophies the genesis of reality is understood in terms of downfall, or of alienation, or of a derivation to be reabsorbed into eternal unity. It is never thought of as a positive creation.

In the biblical tradition, on the contrary, and this is an element of its originality, the genesis of reality is a truly positive act, an act of creation. This complete reversal of the very basis of metaphysical thought carries tremendous consequences. From the very beginning, starting from this fundamental point of all metaphysics, Hebrew thought runs in a direction opposite to the current of Greek thought, mounts the slope which the Greeks and their modern followers descend since the latter deem all tangible stuff to be born from a *decline*, a degradation, while the Hebrew considers it the result of an *ascent*, the result of a truly positive act: creation.

When we consider the unanimity with which philosophers from the earliest days have pronounced the genesis of reality a negative movement, when we see that in modern times they have still preferred the theory of fall, inversion or alienation, we might well wonder whether the human mind suffers from some constitutional incapacity — a sort of second law of thermodynamics of the mind, immanent in intelligence — which prevents us from grasping what creation is, though we witness its reality endlessly, in the smallest blade of grass which opposes the second principle — by growing.

Bergson believed this.

It is to his valuable analyses that we shall turn, in seeking to uncover and stress the originality of the Hebrew trends of thought on these specific points: the fundamental notion of creation, and the related notion of time, the Hebrews' conception of history as a maturing growth, their understanding of the organic, of the organic development of reality, and finally, perhaps, the biblical meaning of eternity.

Bergson made his departure from a positive study of psychological and biological fact. His conclusions lead in a direction opposite to that of the metaphysics of antiquity. In Bergson's own words, he goes up the slope which they descend.

Brought about by a scientific analysis of living reality, this reversal of the currents of thought established by the Greek philosophers coincides with the spontaneous orientation of Hebrew thought which also runs counter to the habits of the Greek intelligence.

* * *

How can anything be added to what is?

"This is the problem so long argued by the old philosophers: how could a multiplicity of any sort, a dyad or a number, come into being out of the One as we have defined him? How is it that the One did not remain within himself?" [1]

There are two ways for the One to become the many.

A unity, a living organism, can turn into a multiplicity through disintegration, through decomposition. This is death, in this case the movement going from the One to the many is negative, it is a fall.

Or else a unity, a seed in this case, can multiply through fertility, growing into an organism which can in turn produce more seed. A definitely positive transformation, this; gain rather than loss, it is genesis in the true sense, a birth.

In the first case, of course, there is actually *less* "after" than there was "before," less in the many than in the living one. In the second case, on the contrary, there is *more* after than before, more in the many than in the one.

Quite often in Greek thought there seems to be an assimilation, or even a confusion of these two dialectics of the One and the many, which nevertheless have nothing in common except from the abstract point of view of number. It looks as if the Greek philosophers, as a result of a natural pessimism, spontaneously linked the multiplicity of living beings to a disintegration, a pulverization of the One. The multitude of living beings represented only something negative, something like a catastrophe.

Not so to the Hebrew. To him the multitude of beings is the result of an eminently positive act, a creation, an excellent creation. Indeed the Creator Himself at every step in the genesis of the many, sees that all this is "very good." Fertility is a blessing, to

---

[1] PLOTINUS, *Enn.* 5: 6.

multiply is to be blessed, for God orders: "Increase, multiply and cover the earth." And the great number of creatures, innumerable as sand and stars, reveal the power, the inexhaustible fruitfulness of the Creator.

Later on we shall see that biblical metaphysics is characterized by the absence of the negative concept of matter. One consequence of this fact is of interest to us now. To Plato and to the Neo-Platonic tradition the One is separated from himself, undone in multiplicity by what they term "*chōra*." With Aristotle, Plato's "*chōra*" is identified with "matter," the principle of individuation. Therefore a negative principle is responsible for the multiplicity of beings.

Biblical metaphysics, by avoiding this negative principle, is able to look upon the genesis of all beings as a positive act, in itself desirable because it is excellent. Individuation, therefore, is no longer to be explained through the intervention of "matter." The explanation lies in the creative act itself, which wills the existence of this or that *particular being*. There is an entirely new meaning to the relations of the one and the many.

* * *

There is, in the universe of the Bible, another aspect of the dialectic of the one and the many which corresponds to the Greek conception of it. Dust, to the Hebrew, corresponds to the Greek idea of the many, the divers, the indeterminate. Dust is the very figure of death, the final outcome of decay, an object of disgust and abomination. A sacrament of mourning, one might say: in days of disaster the Jews would throw dust on their heads as a sign of affliction. [1]

"You shall walk on your belly and you shall eat dust all the days of your life," [2] God tells the serpent. Which recalls the psalmist's cry: "dust is my bread." [3]

Death which awaits us, which inhabits us, is our potential of returning to dust: "...until you return into the earth from which you were taken. For you are dust and you will return to dust." [4] *'ereṣ*, earth, often designates hell, (the Assyrian *ersitu*, the sheol): "those who turn from me are inscribed on the earth." [5]

---

[1] Jos. 7: 6; Neh. 9: 1; Job 16: 15; Amos 2: 7. Cf. Apoc. 18: 19.
[2] Gen. 3: 14.   [3] Ps. 102: 10.
[4] Gen. 3: 19; Eccl. 3: 19; Ps. 103: 14.   [5] Jer. 17: 13.

"Those who dwell in houses of mud, who have their foundations in dust, who are reduced to powder." [1]   "Soon I shall sleep in the dust." [2]   "You molded me like clay and you would bring me back to dust." [3]   "If he recalled to him his spirit and his breath all flesh would expire instantly and man would return to dust." [4]   "You reduce me to the dust of death." [5]   "Dust returns to the earth according to its former state." [6]   "Those who go down into the dust, those who cannot prolong their lives." [7]

"Awake and sing, you who are laid in the dust, for your dew is a dew of light and earth will give up the dead." [8]   Daniel refers to the dead in the same manner: "many of those who sleep in the dust will awaken." [9]

Despair, which is an anticipation of death, is expressed by the presence of dust: "soul is bound to the dust.   Give me back my life according to your word." [10]   The liturgy of mourning — sackcloth and ashes — pictures despair: "I have sewn a sack to my skin, I have rolled my forehead in the dust." [11]   "Our soul is sunk down into the dust, our belly is stuck to the ground." [12]

The very contrary of this dust of death, this despairful multiplicity, is *the* One, the Living who gives life, the Only from whom all unity proceeds, *'eḥad*.   And so indeed we find a dialectic of the many and the one in many ways similar to the Greek dialectic. We shall examine later their essential difference: to the Greek the one and the many are two constituent principles which build the world; the diverse, *apeiron*, is bound together and given shape by the one, *sundesmos*.   In the Hebrew world, on the contrary, there are not two principles to being, there is one only, God.   Dust is not a constitutive element of the world like the *matter* of things. It is the result, rather, of a tendency: death.   *Dust is not cause of death, but it is death which fathers dust.*   In fact dust is merely the result and image of an evil cosmic tendency, it is not a principle of being.   For the only principle of being is Yhwh. *   Dust is

---

[1] Job 4: 19.
[2] Job 7: 21.
[3] Job 10: 9.
[4] Job 34: 14; Ps. 104: 29.
[5] Ps. 22: 16; Cf. 90: 3.
[6] Eccl. 12: 7.
[7] Ps. 22: 30.
[8] Is. 26: 19.
[9] Dan. 12: 2.
[10] Ps. 119: 25.
[11] Job 16: 15.
[12] Ps. 44: 26.

* We choose to spell Yhwh, as in the Hebrew, in order to stress that this is not the exotic name of some oriental divinity, but truly the Name that has a meaning. Meaning, not sound, makes it the Name of God.   "Hoc nomen *Qui est* maxime proprium nomen Dei propter sui significationem.   Non enim significat formam aliquam; sed ipsum esse."   *St. Thomas, Sum. Theol. Ia, q. XIII, a. xi.*

a later and possibly an accidental disintegration of the created. It does not precede creation. In other words, and this is one of the fundamental differences between Greek and Hebrew thought, the universe of the Bible is not dualistic.

* * *

From the Platonist and the Neo-Platonist point of view any move from the one to the many, any generation, is essentially a degradation and a fall.

To Plotinus procession must necessarily be a downward movement. "...All beings that attain the perfect state engender. So the ever perfect being ever engenders. He engenders a being lesser than himself." [1]

"...A complete being must engender and so great a power must not remain sterile. But neither can it be, in this case, that the engendered being be superior. As an image of the generator he is inferior to him." [2]

"...That which comes from him (from the One) must not be identical to him nor superior to him; for what is superior to the One who is beyond everything else? Consequently it must be inferior, in other words less perfect. What is less perfect than the One? It is the not-one, therefore the many...." [3]

"...Engendered beings cannot rise. Instead they are constantly descending by a degree and increasing in number." *

From the foregoing it is clear that to the Neo-Platonist the procession of the Son must necessarily be a degradation of sorts, the Son *must* be inferior to the Father. ** Christian theology, on the contrary, maintains the equality of the Son and the Father.

---

[1] PLOTINUS, *Enn.* 5: 1, 6.
[2] PLOTINUS, *Enn.* 5: 1, 7; 5: 8, 1; 5: 2, 2.
[3] PLOTINUS, *Enn.* 5: 3, 15.

* To Plotinus, multiplication which is spatialization, is a degradation: "For the more beauty goes towards matter in extending itself in space, the more it weakens, the more it becomes inferior to the beauty that remains in unity. Everything that disperses itself, whether physical energy, or heat, or strength, or even beauty, by this fact does separate itself from itself." (*Enn.* 5, 8, 1).

** This is an exact explanation of the genesis and the success of arianism. It is an attempt at an easy explanation of the Incarnation within the framework of Greek philosophy.

Within a metaphysics of biblical origin generation does not necessarily imply degradation. A being may very well generate its equal.

* * *

"Spinoza rejects the idea of an absolute creation and replaces it by the idea of a necessary production of the world by God." This necessary production of the world "is to be compared to the deduction of properties enclosed in a notion...." [1] In Spinoza's words: "Ex necessitate divinae naturae infinita infinitis modis (hoc est omnia, quae sub intellectum infinitum cadere possunt) sequi debent."   Demonstration: "Haec Propositio unicuique manifesta esse debet, si modo ad hoc attendat, quod ex data cujuscumque rei definitione plures proprietates intellectus concludit, quae revera ex eadem (hoc est, ipsa rei essentia) necessario sequuntur, et eo plures, quo plus realitatis rei definitio exprimit, hoc est, quo plus realitatis rei definitae essentia involvit." [2]

"Verum ego me satis clare ostendisse puto (vid. Prop. 16), a summa Dei potentia, sive infinita natura, infinitis modis, hoc est, omnia necessario effluxisse, vel semper eadem necessitate sequi; eodem modo ac ex natura trianguli ab aeterno et in aeternum sequitur, ejus tres angulos aequeri duobus rectis." [3]

The idea of creation is a pseudo-concept to Spinoza, an idea which implies contradiction: "Demonstravi (vid. Coroll. Prop. 6

---

[1] V. DELBOS, *Le Spinozisme,* p. 175.

[2] SPINOZA, *Eth.* 1, prop. 16.   From the necessity of the divine nature must follow an infinite number of things in infinite ways — that is, all things which can fall within the sphere of infinite intellect.

Proof. — This proposition will be clear to everyone who remembers that from the given definition of anything the intellect infers several properties, which really necessarily follow therefrom (that is, from the actual essence of the thing defined); and it infers more properties in proportion as the definition of the thing expresses more reality, that is, in proportion as the essence of the thing defined involves more reality. (Translated in: THE PHILOSOPHY OF BENEDICT DE SPINOZA, by R.H.M. Elwes, Tudor Publishing Co., New York.)

[3] SPINOZA, *Eth.* 1, prop. 17, schol.   However, I think I have shown sufficiently clearly (by Prop. XVI), that from God's supreme power, or infinite nature, an infinite number of things — that is, all things, have necessarily flowed out in an infinite number of ways, or always follow from the same necessity; in the same way as from the nature of a triangle it follows from eternity and for eternity, that its three inferior angles are equal to two right angles. (Prop. XVII, Schol. Transl. by R.H.M. Elwes, *loc. cit.*)

et Schol. 2 Prop. 8), nullam substantiam ab alio posse produci vel creari." [1]

"...si quis statuat, substantiam creari, simul statuit, ideam falsam factam esse veram, quo sane nihil absurdius concipi potest." [2]

Hence it follows that: "Res particulares nihil sunt, nisi Dei attributorum affectiones, sive modi, quibus Dei attributa certo et determinato modo exprimuntur." [3]

Bergson, in his writings, and in his lectures on Spinoza given at the Collège de France, explicitly professed a conception quite contrary to that of Spinoza in regard to the idea of creation. Bergson is the first among philosophers to have rediscovered the metaphysical reality, the positive significance of creation in its temporal aspect.   In this sense he continues the basic tradition of the mediaeval theologians' Christian philosophy.

"Everything about the idea of creation will appear obscure as long as we think of *things* being created and a *thing* which creates. Such is our usual manner of thought and our understanding cannot prevent itself from proceeding in this manner...

"Creation... is not a mystery. We experience it in our own selves as soon as we act freely. It is no doubt absurd to say that new things add themselves to things already extant, since any *thing* is the result of a solidification effected by our understanding, and since there are never any other *things* beside those constituted by our understanding. To speak of things that are created would mean to say that understanding gives itself more than it gives itself — *in se* a contradictory affirmation, a vain and empty imagination. But that action should increase as it advances, that action should create throughout its progress, is something that each one of us observes when he looks at himself in action." [4]

* * *

---

[1] SPINOZA, *Eth.* I, prop. 15, schol.   I have demonstrated... (see Corol. Prop. 6 and Schol. 2, Prop. 8), that no substance can be produced or created by another being. (Prop. 15, Schol. translated in SPINOZA SELECTIONS, John Wild, Charles Scribner's Sons, New York.)

[2] SPINOZA, *Eth.* I, prop. 8, schol. II.   ... if anyone affirmed that substance is created, it would be the same as saying that a false idea was true — in short, the height of absurdity. (Prop. VII, Schol. II, transl. R.H.M. Elwes, *loc. cit.*)

[3] SPINOZA, *Eth.* I, prop. 15, Coroll. Individual things are nothing but affections or modes of God's attributes, expressing those attributes in a certain and determinate manner. (Prop. 25, Corol. translated by John Wild, *op. cit.*)

[4] BERGSON, *L'Evolution créatrice,* pp. 249-250, Presses Universitaires de France, 1946.

Only the Hebrew tradition energetically asserts the *creation* of reality. It alone uncompromisingly affirms the goodness of reality, of the sensible world, of created things. *Valde bonum*, says Genesis, "The world is very good." The idea of creation implies a) that there is a basic distinction between the creator and the created, and b) that the creator himself is transcendent.

Are not these two propositions related?

It would seem that the two contrary assertions were similarly connected. First: no distinction between God and the world in consequence of the absence of the idea of creation; second: a pessimistic view of the sensible world. The sensible, "matter," "body," are by nature an enslavement of the soul. Existence in this world is an exile; the body is a tomb; the soul's "incorporation" a downfall; the many are a degradation of the One; becoming and time are a downgrade course, a fall from unchangeableness and eternity. Thus Plato: "It is impossible that evil should disappear, Theodorus, for there will always necessarily be a contrary to good. It is just as impossible that evil should have its place among the gods. So mortal nature and this nether region fatally must be the ground over which evils run their course. From this we see in what direction we should strive: from here below to there above, the promptest possible escape *(fugē)*. To escape is to become like God, so far as possible." [1] Plotinus also, often evokes this theme of flight. [2]

The narrative of Genesis distinguishes the Creator from the created and the creation from the fall. On the contrary, and characteristically, Gnostic pantheisms make no such distinctions: Creator is creation, creation is fall. These two confusions are linked in logic; one calls for the other.

In trying to explain the origin of evil the unprompted mind appears to lay the blame spontaneously on the process of genesis itself: and, if we deny creation, genesis is, in fact, the fall of God himself. Genesis and fall are seen as one, the origin of evil and the origin of being are confounded, and the primal fall, the scission from which the world was born, must lie in God. The many are a degradation, a scattering of the one, and the tangible and varied world is therefore, by its very nature, a place of exile and alienation. The sensible, like a scapegoat, is made to bear the blame for the origin of evil. "Matter" is at fault.

---

[1] PLATO, *Theat.*, 176a.
[2] PLOTINUS, cf. *Enn.* I: 6, 8; 6: 9, 11.

If creation and fall are one, or rather if they are not distinguished (being mingled by a sort of osmosis) then salvation is to *turn back* towards that origin which is beyond the generation of the many. It is a flight, a deliverance from the body-prison, a purification from the body's contact. *

In contributing the idea of creation, biblical tradition distinguishes it very clearly (in the same chapter of Genesis) from the idea of fall. We do not find here any necessary link between the origin of evil and the origin of being. Creation is "very good." Such a distinction opens a new perspective upon the problem of evil. Since the origin of evil is not to be found in the act of creation, we discover in regard to the sensible world an attitude quite different from that of the Greek thinker. The "sensible," "matter," the "body," these are not evil and sinful.

All things created are excellent. Nothing is impure in itself. The origin of evil is situated elsewhere than in the sensible world. It is not a "soul's" presence in a "body" which is sin, for sin is of another order; sin has a spiritual origin. The typical sin is falsehood.

By transporting the problem of evil to this new level biblical tradition transforms the whole perspective of the problem. While the outlook on this level reveals a greater depth of tragedy, the sensible world is still seen with much more optimism. It is, we have said, a most excellent world. Natural thought underestimated the real tragedy. If the sensible was evil's cause it would suffice to flee from it; ascetic practice and a natural mysticism would suffice.

In the biblical problematic salvation is not found in ascetic practice. That would be too simple, "...I do not ask you to withdraw them from the world, but to preserve them from evil." [1] As the problem of evil takes a new form, so does the conception of salvation. In its new form this conception is properly spiritual, supernatural.

---

* Neo-Platonic conversion is an *epistrophē*, a movement of return to the One. It is accomplished by abolition of the multiple delivering the soul from care and from alienation in the body's matter. One could almost call it a spatial movement if it did not precisely consist in a suppression of space as well as of time.

Bibilical and Christian conversion are a *metanoia*, that is to say, according to the expression of St. Paul, a "newness of mind" (Rom. 12: 2), what the Old Testament called a renewal of the heart. It is a spiritual conversion.

Neo-Platonic conversion is effected by asceticism and by a solitary effort of the soul. Christian conversion is the combined work of God and of man. It is supernatural. No asceticism can replace the supernatural, spiritual virtues of faith and charity.

[1] John 15: 15.

The Gnostic who returns to the ancient Greek, Platonic problematic, confuses what the biblical revelation distinguishes, the creation and the fall, and correlatively salvation and asceticism. The Manicheism of the Catharists carries with it a conception of salvation which rejects Christian supernaturalism.

Although, to the Gnostic the creation is a fall, the fall (original sin) is not really an evil but, *felix culpa*, an indispensable element in the becoming of the world, of history, and even in the becoming of God Himself. For God, out of this tragic adventure to which He submits brings about His birth into a higher and unalienable joy. Original joy was immediate. Final plenitude, having undergone the mediation of evil and surmounted the dissonance which tore it asunder, will no longer be subject to the temptation of exile.

Evil is not "foreign to the divine essence," [1] Hegel writes. "The absolute plays out this tragedy with himself eternally. He eternally engenders himself into objectivity; in this concrete shape he delivers himself to passion and to death and is reborn from his ashes into his majesty." [2]

The original fall is the scission which set off the march of history, "the calvary of the absolute spirit... without which he would be a lifeless solitude." [3]

According to Gnostic Pantheism God tore Himself asunder, * dispersed Himself, exiled Himself (cf. the Cabala's exile of the Shekhina), alienated Himself (cf. Hegel's *Entfremdung*), in order to win the joy of rediscovering Himself beyond this odyssey, the

---

[1] HEGEL, *Die Phänomenologie des Geistes.*
[2] HEGEL, *Werke*, Lasson edition, VII, p. 384.
[3] HEGEL, *Die Phänomenologie des Geistes.*
* The idea that at the origin there already existed a schism, a scission, and that it is this *Entzweiung* which is responsible for the genesis of reality, can already be found in Plotinus. Cf. for instance, *Enn.* 6: 7, 39; 3: 7, 11.
  To this is added the idea that this separation is the work of conscience, of intelligence; cf. *Enn.* 6: 7, 39: "And that is why (Plato) is right to place alterity with intelligence."
  Conscience = schism, *apostasis: Enn.* 5: 8, 11.
  In the Cabala understanding is also the cause of separation: "The name of that Seripha, *Bina,* can be taken to mean, not only 'intelligence,' but also 'that which divides things among themselves,' in other words, differentiation." (SCHOLEM, *The Major Trends of Jewish Mysticism.*)
  Concerning the development of this idea in German romanticism and particularly in Hegel's philosophy, cf. J. WAHL, *Le malheur de la conscience dans la philosophie de Hegel.*

richer for having surmounted the mediation of negativity which He Himself willed. "The life of God and divine knowledge can therefore, if one wishes, be expressed as a game of love with Himself. But this idea sinks to edification and even to insipidity when lacking the seriousness, suffering, patience and labor of the negative." [1]

Pantheism does not follow out its intuition to the end. It does not go so far as to think that God, for His own joy and for His glory, created beings that are really distinct from Him, autonomous beings that are in fact gods, in the sense that it is written: "You are gods."

Pantheism nullifies the act of creation, evacuates it, atrophies it. In place of creation the Pantheist gnoses, from Neo-Platonism down to Hegel, conceive of a weak, a shrunken scheme. None of these theories quite dared to imagine that God had carried paradox to the point of creating liberties other than His own; that God had risked creating other gods *because* "it is His pleasure to be with the children of men."

It is in this bold act that the full dimensions of the biblical revelation come to view. The natural scope of human conceptions never reached so far. Gnostic heresies sin out of sorrow. They dare not accept all the revealed but reduce it to the measure of their deficient hopes. The idea of creation is too "hard," "*Skleros ho logos.*"

* * *

To analyse the metaphysical positions of Hebrew biblical thought is to make an inventory of the content and implications of the idea of creation; to distinguish this idea from all that it is not, (from fabrication, properly a human activity), and to develop all its requirements and all its consequences.

We shall observe how this metaphysical system, to which the key is the idea of creation, has its own particular inner coherence, just as we might demonstrate the inevitable logical consequences of the absence or rejection of this idea in the philosophies which ignore or deny it.

---

[1] HEGEL, *Die Phänomenologie des Geistes*, Lasson Edition, p. 20.

If one does not accept the idea of creation, with all its implications one is brought by logical necessity to reject:

time;

the concept of *person*, since the many was not engendered by a creator's will, proceeding instead from a purely negative individuation by "matter";

the concept of *love*, since the great number of persons is but the unfortunate and illusory reverse of a oneness which alone is real. What the Pantheist calls love can only be the return to the One.

Nor can we any longer speak of God's love for His creatures, for "there cannot in any true sense be love of God for another being since all that *is* forms but one single thing, to wit, God Himself." [1]

Creation, and time, and the concepts of person and of love have always eluded modern philosophers as they eluded the ancients. They are truly a contribution of biblical tradition, the object of a Christian philosophy.

---

[1] SPINOZA, *Brief Treatise*, chap. 23.

chapter two

TIME

The moment of creation is not far removed from us, lost in an unfathomable past.   Today, as in the beginning, creation continues. More accurately, we might say, today also *is* a beginning. Far from having ended, coming-to-be continues to this day.   We are in becoming.

Spinoza may have thought the notion of creation an absurdity, still it remains a constant, daily fact in our experience.   Throughout the world, at every moment, we witness creation.   If we restrict the creative act to the first moment of history we are forced to admit that nothing was created since and that reality thenceforth has merely been a frozen repetition of the first inventive act.   In this way we would confuse creation and fabrication. *   The act of fabrication is completed all at once and with experience can be performed in an ever shorter time.   But reality is not a universe of fabricated objects, once and for all perfected.   Our world is even now being engendered.   By definition creation is not fabrication.

This act of creation is the most common, the most universal experimental fact, the richest in metaphysical implications. Something new is brought into being which in no manner existed before.   Such is the significance of the concept of *time*.

"Time" is a concept which implies that the whole of reality did not appear at once; it means that there is a progressive and incessant creation of new reality, that the real is engaged in making itself, little by little it is improvised; it means that something *new* is being engendered continually.   A concept derived from reality, it

---

* We use "fabricate," "fabrication" in their somewhat archaic sense of "to make, to manufacture" that implies the organization of a given material. (*Translator's note*).

characterizes the continuous parturition of the universe. Time is a concept which, through one of its properties, connotes the act of creation.

⁕ ⁕ ⁕

The verb *bara*, to create, is used 48 times in the Old Testament; 20 times in the second Isaiah, 11 times in Genesis (the Sacerdotal Code), 6 times in the Psalms and 3 times in Ezekiel. In every instance God is the subject. *Bara* is an action of God alone. The verb is reserved for Him.

The distinction between the divine manner of making which is creation, and the human manner of making, which is fabrication, is of fundamental importance in metaphysics. This distinction is already to be found in language itself. *Solius Dei est creare.*

Bara designates divine action insofar as it produces the new or the renewed. "Yhwh has *created* a new thing on earth." [1] "Behold I *create new* heavens and a *new* earth." [2] "O God, *create* in me a pure heart, and *renew* a firm spirit within me." [3]

In the New Testament we find the same awareness of the apparition of new things through the act of creation: "Behold I shall make all things new" *(Idou kaina poiō panta).* [4]

But time which is the growth of all that is new, also implies super-annuation and extinction. Certain realities lose their actuality, and a fixation on what is past is an inversion, a misunderstanding of temporal creation. "The old things are past, see, everything has been made new." [5]

Under this plan, this temporal "economy" of creation, there is an old man [6] and a new creature *(kainē ktisis)* [7] which is the inner man.

Creation, like sap in a tree, always works from within: "even as the outer man wanes, the inner man *renews* himself from day to day... [8] so that we walk in newness of life *(en kainotēti zoēs)...* in newness of spirit and not in obsolescence of letter." [9]

We shall see later (Part III), how important is this temporal understanding of creation in defining the biblical concepts of

---

[1] Jer. 31: 22; Cf. Num. 16: 30.
[2] Is. 65: 17; Cf. Is. 4: 5.
[3] Ps. 51: 12.
[4] Apoc. 21: 5.
[5] 2 Cor. 5: 17.
[6] Rom. 6: 6.
[7] 2 Cor. 5: 17; Gal. 6: 15.
[8] 2 Cor. 4: 16.
[9] Rom. 6: 4.

intelligence (a dynamic intuition of the growth of being), and of stupidity (an inversion, a sin against creation, an infantile fixation upon the obsolete and the dead).

***

To create means to create *newness*.   Creation is not fabrication. It is not to make the same from the same (which is the manner of fabrication).   The apparition of the new is the specific sign of creation. Its definition can only be approached apophatically, by clearing it of all that it is not and distinguishing it clearly from the human manner of making, fabrication.

This intuition of the *new*, this sensitive awareness of its metaphysical import was Bergson's living and original insight. "Reality appears to us a ceaseless springing up of new things." [1]

The basic intuition of Bergson's philosophy, the sounding of which his whole philosophy is an inventory, seems to have been an encounter (*epaphē*, Plotinus called it) with the act of creation, immanent in reality, a feel for what the act of creation is in its metaphysical originality.   It is an apprehension of that being of things, * that act of being which is an act of creation (*esse* which is a *creare*).   For being is not only a "position" as Kant called it — only the *dasein* of "things," of fabricated objects, is a "position" — being is not static but a creative act immanent in the created, to the extent that the latter is still alive.   Being is an operative, inventive act, innovating endlessly because the end of innovation means the end of being, and any interruption is already an inversion.   The act of being calls up "perpetual flow of unpredictable novelty."   Being is always an act of genius. To "create new things" and to "create" mean the same thing. In fact, the first term is redundant.   Only fabrication is repetitious. Bergson's ontology returns to a clear awareness of the *being of created reality*, whereas too often philosophers, especially since Descartes, deal only with the *being of "things,"* that is to say, of fabricated objects, so forging the factitious ontology of a dead universe.

Creation is continuous within us and about us.   True, Descartes speaks of a continued creation, but to him these words represent

---

[1] BERGSON, *L'Evolution créatrice*, p. 47, P.U.F. 1946.
* "Esse, quod est magis intimum cuilibet et quod profundius omnibus inest" (St. Thomas).

merely the permanence of the primaeval *fiat*: God has not repudiated
His command; He subscribes to it up to this day. The "continued
creation" of Descartes is not a constant *invention* of new realities,
but a conservation of what already exists. "Conservation and
creation differ only in respect to our way of thinking, they do not
differ in fact." [1] It is not an act that continues to innovate, it is an
act that repeats itself. Duration, in the philosophy of Descartes
is permanence, not invention. For creation to him is a creation
of *things (res)*, [2] as opposed to beings; and "things" once they
are "created" need only to be "preserved." We do not find here
a notion of creation continuing its work immanent in the created.
Descartes' world is a world of things. His creation differs very
little from fabrication.

While continued creation in Descartes is the identity of the
same act which persists, in the biblical world and in Bergson
"creation appears no longer as simply continued but as continuous." [3]
The creative act continues to invent. We have not yet reached
the seventh day: genesis continues. "We can feel that reality
is a perpetual growth, a creation which goes on endlessly." [4]
"The universe is not made, but makes itself unceasingly." [5] In
the language of Teilhard de Chardin, there is no static cosmos;
there is only cosmogenesis. "For we know that the whole of creation
to this day is moaning and bearing in common the pangs of
childbirth." [6] "My father is at work to this day" *(ho patēr mou
heōs arti ergazetai)*. [7]

Cartesian time is made up of a dust of instants. It is discontinuous
and syncopated because in fact it does not exist. Time has no
function — no directional flow — since creation does not really
continue inventively, but merely maintains itself, that is, repeats
itself. In such a universe things are forever in danger of falling
back to nothingness, except that the Divine will uphold them and
prevent them from vanishing back into the original void. *

---

[1] DESCARTES, IIIe *Médit*. Adam Tannery Ed., t. IX, p. 39.
[2] Cf. DESCARTES, IIIe *Méd*. AT, t. VII, p. 49.
[3] BERGSON, *L'Evolution créatrice*, p. 345, P.U.F. 1946.
[4] BERGSON, *L'Evolution créatrice*, p. 240, P.U.F. 1946.
[5] BERGSON, *L'Evolution créatrice*, p. 242, P.U.F. 1946.
[6] Rom. 8: 22.   [7] John 5: 17.
* This "schizophrenia" of Cartesian time can be understood because, in the
words of Mr. Jean Wahl, "according to this conception of time, time has no
positive action."   J. WAHL, *Du rôle de l'idée d'instant dans la philosophie de
Descartes*, Paris, 1920, p. 25.   So we reach this paradox: "...Creation is
continuous because duration is not."   *(Ibid.*, p. 18).

"...Philosophy has never frankly admitted this continuous creation of unforeseeable novelty. Such a thought was already repugnant to the ancients because, being more or less Platonists, they imagined that Being was given, once and for all, complete and perfect, in the immutable system of Ideas: hence the world which unfolds itself before our eyes could add nothing to it; this world, on the contrary, was but a diminution or a degradation; its successive states measured the widening or narrowing gap between what is, a shadow projected in time, and what should be, the Idea seated in eternity.... It was Time that spoiled everything." [1] "None of (the philosophers) has attempted to find positive attributes to time. They consider succession to be an imperfect form of coexistence, and duration to be a privation of eternity. That is why, no matter what they do, they cannot conceive radical newness and unforeseeability." [2]

To modern metaphysics as to the metaphysics of the ancients, "reality, like truth, was wholly given in eternity. Both dislike the idea of a reality which would come to be progressively, that is to say, at bottom, the idea of an absolute duration." [3] "It is precisely because it is always trying to reconstruct, and to reconstruct with what is already given, that intelligence allows all that is new at every moment of a history to escape it. It does not admit the unpredictable. It rejects all creation." [4]

"As regards invention itself, our intelligence cannot catch it in its *springing forth*, that is to say, in its aspect of unpredictability, nor in its *genius*, that is to say, in its aspect of creativity. To explain creation is always to reduce it, the unforeseeable and the new to old or familiar elements arranged merely in a different order. Intelligence can no more accept complete newness than it can accept radical *becoming*. This means that intelligence here again misses an essential aspect of life...." [5]

Bergson expressed his intuition of the creative act in terms of the derived concept which is time: * "Duration... a continuous

---

[1] BERGSON, *Le possible et le réel*, in *La Pensée et le Mouvant*, p. 115, P.U.F. 1946.
[2] *Ibid.*, p. 10.
[3] BERGSON, *L'Evolution créatrice*, p. 353, P.U.F. 1946.
[4] BERGSON, *L'Evolution créatrice*, p. 164, P.U.F. 1946.
[5] BERGSON, *L'Evolution créatrice*, p. 165, P.U.F. 1946.
* "A philosophy that sees in duration the very material of reality." (*L'Evolution créatrice*, p.272, P.U.F.1946). The word "duration" may have misled Bergson. It can too easily evoke the Heraclitan image of the flowing river, *panta rei*. But the water that we see downstream already pre-existed upstream. All was given

creation, an uninterrupted springing up of newness." [1]   "The universe lasts. The more we delve into the nature of time, the more we shall understand that duration means invention, the creation of forms, a constant elaboration of the absolutely new." [2]   "While the ancient conception of scientific knowledge always ended by making time a degradation and change the diminution of a Form given from all eternity, the new conception, followed to its end, would, on the contrary, lead one to view time as a progressive increase of the absolute, and the evolution of things as a continuous invention of new forms." [3]   "Time is invention or it is nothing at all." [4]

"How is it that all was not given at once?.... If the future is condemned to follow the present instead of being given along with it, it is because endlessly (in time) the unforeseeable and the new are being created." [5]

Time is not only a succession, if by this word we mean a juxtaposition of events, one after another, like a juxtaposition of objects in space.   Such a succession would only be a transposition of spatial coexistence in the shape of a one-way line.   Time is an invention, a creative genesis of new being which in no way pre-existed.   It could not be symbolized by a line.

Nor is time a receptacle: "When we think of time as a homogenous milieu where states of consciousness appear to unfold, we thereby conceive the whole of it at once, which means that we take duration out of it.   This reflection should warn us that we are unconsciously falling back on space." [6]

* * *

Within a metaphysical system in which the world is but an image of the intelligible from which it proceeds by participation,

---

from the start.   Once again the specific aspect of creation, time, is done away with and betrayed by a spatial image.   Of course, it may well be the essence of an image to be spatial.   Bergson lent himself to confusion with Heraclitism by some of his expressions: "the flux of time," "things which flow off," "reality which flows off," "the essence of reality is that it flows."   etc.

[1] BERGSON, *La Pensée et le Mouvant*, p. 9, P.U.F. 1946.
[2] BERGSON, *L'Evolution créatrice*, p. 11, P.U.F. 1946.
[3] BERGSON, *L'Evolution créatrice*, p. 343, P.U.F. 1946.
[4] BERGSON, *L'Evolution créatrice*, p. 341, P.U.F. 1946.
[5] BERGSON, *L'Evolution créatrice*, p. 339, P.U.F. 1946.
[6] BERGSON, *Essai sur les Données Immédiates de la Conscience*, p. 73, P.U.F. 1946.

there can only be an imitation of the eternal Idea, but no real creation of new being. Time itself, in such a case, is but a "moving imitation of eternity." [1]

If the genesis of the sensible and the multiple is effected by a fall from the one, time is but the measure of this degradation, it is negative, it represents a fall: *katebē chronos;* [2] *exepese chronos.* [3]

If creation is nothing but "the necessary deduction of properties enclosed in a notion," [4] then time is nonexistent, since a deduction, in all rigor — that is in the case of an infinite mind — could be an instantaneous operation. "Existence would be the coexistence of essences in so far as they cannot be brought back to unity; time would be the sum of obstacles encountered by eternity." [5] "Spinoza does not believe in time." [6]

But if creation is an effective action, truly and progressively generative of new being, then time will be its positive measure.

* * *

Our definition of time will vary according to our conception of movement. We are aware of three kinds of movement: displacement, cycle, and evolution.

First, displacement. This is the most factitious of the three, the movement of fabricated objects or of "things" cut off from the organic whole which engendered them. It is the poorest movement, secondary, degraded, derived from an earlier one. Philosophers have unfortunately too often considered only this type of movement, the movement typical of billiard balls, the displacement of "things." One may very well ask whether the problems related to causality and finality do not arise from having been proposed in the artificial universe of fabricated objects.

Two, the cyclic movement. Within an organic whole, an astronomical system, or a biological organism, cycles repeat themselves. Whereas a movement of displacement is always reversible, a cyclic movement must be a continuous repetition.

Three, the movement of evolution. This movement is by definition irreversible. It is the movement of maturing, of genesis, of growth.

---

[1] PLATO, *Timaeus* 37 d.   [2] PLOTINUS, *Enn.* 3: 7, 7.
[3] PLOTINUS, *Enn.* 3: 7, 11.   [4] V. DELBOS, *op. cit.*, p. 175.
[5] BERGSON, unpublished course quoted in *Revue Métaphysique et Morale,* 1949.
[6] *Ibid.*

Evolution is the realest, most fundamental movement, that of organic *wholes* in process of development. All other movement, displacement or cycle, is derived from this one. A tree will grow, life will produce new species, the universe will branch out explosively in sheaves, man will be born and will grow: these are *their most essential movements*. An object's displacement is but a secondary phenomenon because a "thing" as such is not a part of living growth, it is life's dross. We shall return to evolutionary movement to see in what form the notion appears in the Bible. But first we should examine the two other kinds of movement.

Displacement is the only movement studied by Descartes. "For my part I know of none other than that which makes a body pass from one place to another by occupying successively all the spaces in between." [1] "Now movement (by which I mean movement from one place to another, for I can conceive only that one, and do not think that one should suppose any other kind in nature), movement I say, therefore, in the sense in which it is usually taken, is nothing but the action by which a body passes from one place to another." [2]

Such a movement is reversible and relative, whereas the movement of evolution is, on the contrary, irreversible and absolute: "And just as we have observed that the same object at the same time changes place and yet does not, so may we say that at the same time it moves and does not move." [3] The world of Descartes, we have said before, is a world of "things," in other words, of fabricated objects. Descartes never understood the nature of the organic. In fact he confused the organic with the mechanical, creation with fabrication. The type of movement examined by Descartes, and after him by Malebranche and by Hume, is, of all movement, the least real and the least instructive. That is why time — and the notions of causality and finality — have been studied in the light of the most unfortunate examples one could possibly choose, the poorest taken from a world of fabricated objects particular to man. This "reistic" conception results from ignorance of physical or biological reality which is always organic.

To this artificial world of dislocated "things," built from a dustlike sum of objects, there corresponds a time composed of unrelated instants. "Descartes considers... as something naturally evident, that time is fundamentally discontinuous, in other words that

---

[1] *Le Monde*, chap. VII, A.T., XI, 39.   [2] *Princ.* II, 24.
[3] *Ibid.*

the present moment depends in no way on the preceding movement." [1]   "The whole time of life can be divided into numberless parts, each one of which in no way depends upon the others." [2]

The Greeks on the other hand, seem to have been especially impressed by cyclic movement, which always runs *within* an evolving system. The movement of creative evolution, on the cosmic or the biological levels, escaped them. It has been remarked that we are only now discovering time. Modern biology, palaeontology and astrophysics, have shown that we are being carried forward in a movement of cosmogenesis on all levels and in every order. But the Greek cosmos is static, complete.

Out of all movements which they could observe, the Greeks noted and gave favored attention to repeating cycles, and to the movement of degradation: katagenesis. "All change," writes Aristotle, "is by its nature an undoing. It is in time that all is engendered and destroyed.... One can see that time itself is the cause of destruction rather than of generation.... For change itself is an undoing; it is indeed only by accident a cause of generation and existence." [3]   Since time is the measure of movement, if movement is negative, time must be negative too: "For we are wont to say that time wears, that all things age in time, all is erased by time, but never that we have learnt or that we have grown young and handsome; for time in itself is more truly a cause of destruction *(phthoras)*, since time is the number of movement, and movement undoes that which is." [4]

And so, just as there are several kinds of movement, and several ways for the one to become the many, so too there are several sorts of time:

(1) the time necessary to deduce from a geometrical figure the properties it contains; at the limit, for an infinite intelligence, this time is equal to zero;

(2) the time taken by an organism's decay; the time for wearing out and disintegrating; a negative time;

(3) the time of a plant's growth, of any living organism's growth; the time of maturation, the time of evolution. This is the yardstick of invention and creation. It is, eminently, positive.

---

[1] Gilson, *Disc. de la Méth. Comm.*, p. 340.
[2] IIIe *Méd.* 53, A.R., VII, 48.
[3] *Phys.* IV, 222 b.   [4] *Ibid.*, 221 a.

As a matter of fact, all those sorts of time, measuring movements of reversible displacement or movements of decay, can be embodied into the only real time, which is that of living reality. "As soon as we return to true duration, we see that it signifies creation, and that, if what is being unmade lasts at all, it can only be through its solidarity with what is being made." [1]

* * *

When they speak of becoming, Greek and Hebrew are not thinking of the same thing.

The Heraclitan "panta rei" means in a sense: all goes away, all escapes us, all flees us. Movement is katagenesis (degradation), time is ageing. The Greek views becoming with pessimism: it is a walk towards death, it bears a negative sign. It is degradation, a downward procession. "The whole of this philosophy which begins with Plato and ends with Plotinus, is the development of a principle which we may set forth thus: "there is more in the immutable than in the moving, one goes from the stable to the unstable by a simple diminution." But it is the contrary which is true." [2]

Greek becoming and Hebrew becoming are affected with contrary signs, they move in opposite directions. The first evokes degradation, descent and fall, everything flows away and undoes itself. The other is ascent and conquest: everything is being created. Platonic and Neo-Platonic becoming represents a dispersion of the One, a loss. The Greeks seem to have been especially impressed by the movements of corruption and dispersal. Biblical becoming shows the fecundity and goodness of the Creator. The Hebrews showed a passionate attention to the process of fecundity, the maturing process. The symbol of the first is the river that flows away irretrievably, or light that loses itself, disperses itself in darkness. The figure of the second is the tree that grows and from one grain becomes a multitude of fruit. In terms of modern physics one might say that Greek thought seems to attach greater importance to entropy, while the Hebrew, without ignoring the cosmic trend to dust, has attached greater importance to the contrary movement, that of "biogenesis," of creation. Biblical time is the measure

---

[1] BERGSON, L'Evolution créatrice, p. 342, P.U.F. 1946.
[2] BERGSON, La Pensée et le Mouvant, p. 217, P.U.F. 1946.

of this parturition, this universal maturing. It is essentially positive and good.

In the biblical texts creation is regarded as an eminently positive reality, the generation of a multitude of beings. Creation is still in progress. As regards man especially, something is still being accomplished, something is still growing. History is this *maturation*.

History is not an eternal flow of unrelated events. It has a beginning *(bereschit)*, and is ordered to an end, just as the tree's growth is ordered to fruitfulness. And so in this maturation of history there are *stages*: "times" and "moments."

It is characteristic of biblical history that those who carry it forward are made aware of its *direction* through the teachings of the prophets. The prophet, the *nabi*, is someone who understands the "sense" of history, what it means and whither it moves. We can understand the "meaning" of a historical event only if we can see what it forebodes. A historical event is a *sign* only in so far as one may read in it what will come of it, just as we can foretell, when the bud appears, that the flower will follow. It is not because of some extrinsic relationship, but very simply because the former actually does produce the latter. The *nabi* is aware of God's creative action and understands those "phases" of it which regard man especially. In this he is like the farmer who knows the "time" of the maturation of his crops. "The king turned to the wise men who had knowledge of the times." [1] "A knowledge of the times to determine what Israel should do." [2]

But the prophet does not see history, stretched out before him like a map, from which he need only pick out individual future events. Such foresight is not the prophet's gift. Rather he sees in which direction events are flowing. This is the scope of prophecy. The Hebrew conception of time excludes any other explanation of it.

It is in the New Testament [3] that we find this awareness of creative time, this sense of the moments of maturation, most acutely present, most precisely expressed. "The time is fulfilled *(peplērōtai ho kairos)*, the kingdom of God is at hand." [4]

In the New Testament two words stand for time. *Kairos* is the time of a certain maturation: "the time of harvest," [5] "the

---

[1] Esth. 1: 13.   [2] 1 Chron. 12: 33.
[3] Cf. O. CULLMANN, *Christ et le Temps*.
[4] Mark: 1: 15.   [5] Matth. 13: 30.

time of fruit." [1]   *Chronos* too is used in relation to genesis or to childbirth: "For Elisabeth the time of childbirth was fulfilled." *

A certain "fullness of time" is necessary for every creation, for the harvest, for childbirth, as for the Incarnation itself: "when the fullness of time came *(to plērōma tou chronou)*, God sent His Son born of a woman." [2]   And it is because the Incarnation is a *birth*, prepared for through centuries by a whole nation, and a whole world, that it could *not* happen at just any time of history. Such moments in which history matures are discernible by intrinsic signs.   Thus the farmer, looking at the grain, can tell the ripeness of the wheat and the approach of harvest: "Do you not yourselves say: yet four more months to harvest? Well, I say to you: lift up your eyes and look at the fields. They are ripe already to harvest." [3]   "Learn this parable of the figtree: as soon as its shoots become tender and the leaves grow, you know that summer is near...." [4]   "Come evening, you say: tomorrow will be fine for the sky is red; and in the morning: today there will be storm for the sky is dark red. You can distinguish the aspects of the sky, but the signs of the time, *(ta semeia tōn kairōn)* you cannot." [5]   "When you see a cloud coming up in the west, you say at once: here comes rain, and so it is. And when you feel the south wind blowing, you say: we will have hot weather.... How is it then that you do not recognize the times that are upon you? *(ton kairon touton pōs ou dokimazete)*." [6]

There is a time for the visitation of God, the *paqad* of God: "because you have not known the time of your visitation..." [7]

Jesus, throughout His life, is aware of a certain maturation, a certain threshhold which must be passed before the acts of His life or death can be accomplished: "My *kairos* has not yet come." [8] "My *kairos* has not yet been fulfilled." [9]   "My time is not yet come." [10] "His time had not yet come." [11]   Later, at a certain moment, Jesus proclaims: "My time, my *kairos*, is near." [12]   "The time has come." [13] "Jesus, knowing that His time had come..." [14]

---

[1] Matth. 21: 34; cf. Matth. 31: 41.
* "A woman when she is in travail has sorrow because her hour is come." Luke 1: 57; cf. John 16: 21.
[2] Gal. 4: 4.   [3] John 4: 35.
[4] Matth. 24: 32.   [5] Matth. 16: 2.
[6] Luke 12: 56.   [7] Luke 19: 44.
[8] John 7: 6.   [9] John 7: 8.
[10] John 2: 4.   [11] John 7: 30; 8: 20.
[12] Matth. 26: 18.   [13] John 12: 23; 17: 1.
[14] John 13: 1.

Just as there was a "time" for the Incarnation, so too there will be a "time" of complete fulfilment, the *plērōma* of all time: the moment of the final maturity of all creation, the time of the definitive harvest. "The time is near at hand." [1] Toward this end the world's growth proceeds according to a plan, an "economy": "the economy of the fulness of time." [2]

History is a constant invention in which innumerable free wills cooperate: the creative action of God and the co-creative action of man. History is not an unfolding in time of a pre-existing model in which all is fore-ordained. For this reason it is impossible to forecast the precise hour of fulfilment: "No one knows the day or the hour of this happening, not even the angels in heaven, no, not even the Son — only the Father." [3] "It is not for you to know the time, *(chronous)*, nor the moments *(kairous)*, that the Father has disposed of in his freedom." [4] Be watchful and awake for you do not know when the moment will come." [5]

Though the hour of plenitude of creation cannot be known, yet, as with all growth, there are discernible signs which indicate the degree of fulfilment, the proximity of the final parturition. "Tell us when these things will happen, and what will be the sign *(to semeion)* of Your coming and of the end of the world?" [*]

"From the figtree learn this parable: when its shoots become tender, and when its leaves grow, you know that summer is near. Likewise, when you see all these things, you will know that (the event) is near at hand, before the very gates." [6]

"Like all things, the world itself has had imperfect beginnings, that white-haired Christian faith might in the end crown its venerable old age. Let those whom this fact perturbs go chide the crops for their tardy ripeness, or the vintage for coming only at year's end, or let them chide the olive because its fruit is the last to ripen." [7]

---

[1] Apoc. 1: 3.   [2] Ephes. 1: 10.
[3] Mark 13: 32.   [4] Acts 1: 7.
[5] Mark 13: 33; cf. Matth. 25: 14.
[*] Matth. 24: 3. Or: of duration; *aiôn* corresponds to the Hebrew *olam*.
[6] Matth. 24: 32; Mark 13: 28; Luke 21: 29.
[7] St. Ambrose, Ep. 18: 28.

chapter three

TIME AND ETERNITY

The analyses of Bergson have been a great help to us in defining the biblical conception of time. Bergson has overthrown the ancient hierarchy between eternity and time. Might not his insight on a more concentrated duration, a creative eternity, help us in understanding the biblical meaning of eternity? and consequently the biblical conception of prophecy?

Eternity, in Hebrew thought as in Bergson, will of course be radically different from the vision of Timaeus or the Third Ennead.

The Greeks conceive eternity primarily as an absence of time How can eternity be accepted where time is not?

* * *

Out of the custom of daily speech, and perhaps also due to the influence of Descartes' conceptions of time and movement, we may tend to think of the present as an infinitesimal particle of time which our consciousness can practically not apprehend in its instantaneous flight. Such a conception of the present is plausible as long as time is a fragmentary sequence of unrelated instants. But if we look upon time as a positive duration the aspect of the present changes and so, as we shall see, does the aspect of eternity. This will appear as we examine the time and eternity of Bergson.

"In the space of a second red light completes 400 trillion successive vibrations. Now red is the color with the greatest wave length, its vibrations therefore are the least frequent.... This single sensation of red light, which we perceive during one second, corresponds in itself to a succession of phenomena which, were they to unfold within our own duration, with the greatest possible economy of time, would occupy more than 250 centuries of our history." [1] In any one of its "instants" our consciousness "encloses thousands of millions of movements which are successive for inert matter, the first of which, were matter able to remember, would appear to the last as an infinitely distant past. When I open my eyes and close them instantly, the sensation of light which I perceive contained within a moment of my time is a condensation of an extraordinarily long history unfolding in the outer world. There, succeeding one another, are trillions of oscillations.... But these events..., which would spread over thirty centuries of a matter become conscious of itself, fill but an instant of my own consciousness which is capable of contracting them." [2]

This experimental fact shows us that "there is not just one rhythm of duration. We may imagine many different rhythms which, slower or faster, would measure the degree of tension, or relaxation, of consciousness and would thus fix their respective stations in the series of beings." [3]

"...Could not all of history be contained in a very short time for a consciousness more extended than our own; a consciousness which could witness the development of humanity and, so to speak, contract it into the great phases of its evolution?" [4] To God a thousand years are as one day.

"...I pronounce the word 'lecture.' Clearly my consciousness grasps the whole word at one time. Were this not so it would not perceive a single word, nor attribute any meaning to it. Yet when I pronounce the last syllable, the first one has already been pronounced; it is something of the past in regard to this one which should therefore be called present. But even this last syllable 'ture' was not pronounced instantaneously... So you cannot draw a line of demarcation between the past and present nor, consequently, between memory and consciousness. When I pronounce the word 'lecture' I have in mind not only the beginning, the middle, and the end of the word, but also the words which preceded it, and further, all the parts of the sentence which I have already pronounced.... Now, had the punctuation of my discourse been different, my sentence might have started earlier; it might have included the preceding sentence, for instance, and my 'present' would have expanded even further into the past. Let us follow

---

[1] BERGSON, *Matière et Mémoire*, pp. 230-231, P.U.F. 1946.
[2] BERGSON, *L'Energie spirituelle*, pp. 15-16, P.U.F. 1946.
[3] BERGSON, *Matière et Mémoire*, p. 232, P.U.F. 1946.
[4] BERGSON, *Matière et Mémoire*, p. 233, P.U.F. 1946.

this reasoning through to the end: let us suppose that my discourse has been going on for years, that from the first awakening of my consciousness it has continued in a single sentence, and let us further suppose that my consciousness is sufficiently detached from the future, sufficiently disinterested in action, to give its exclusive attention to understanding the meaning of this sentence: in such a case I would no more look for an explanation of the complete preservation of this sentence, than I do seek one for the survival of the first syllable of the word 'lecture' when I pronounce the last." [1]   What requires an explanation is not memory but forget-fulness.   Our condition of corporal beings, swept off in action, preoccupied with many cares, is the cause of our forgetfulness. For it is care which crumbles time within our consciousness. "A sufficiently powerful attention to life, enough detached from practical interests, could enclose in an undivided present the entire past history of the conscious person." [2]

Yet contemplative detachment here is not, as in Platonism, an exclusion of action.   On the contrary, a consciousness capable of enclosing history within the grasp of a single thought would have to be eminently active, creative, taut.   But its action would be free from practical cares.   Such a consciousness is not an artisan working on matter but a creator inventing it.   Would not the tension of a conscious being's duration be the measure of its power to act, of the quantity of free and creative activity that it can bring into the world?" [3]

Time connotes the act of creation.   Eternity is the creator's point of view.

We do therefore find in Bergson's philosophy a notion of eternity, taken in the sense that the whole past can, by a free and creative consciousness, be enclosed in an eternal present.   "...We are moving to an ever tauter, tighter, more intense duration at the limit of which would be eternity." [4]   But, one might say, an eternity *a parte ante* and not *a parte post*.   Eternity to Plotinus encloses, *tota simul*, past, present and future.   To Bergson, on the contrary, the future is not included in eternity, and for a very good reason; the future in no way exists, not even in a state of pure possibility. The gates of the future are wide open: it remains *to be created*.

---

[1] BERGSON, *L'Energie spirituelle*, pp. 55-56, P.U.F. 1946.
[2] BERGSON, *La Pensée et le Mouvant*, p. 170, P.U.F. 1946.
[3] BERGSON, *L'Energie spirituelle*, p. 17, P.U.F. 1946.
[4] BERGSON, *La Pensée et le Mouvant*, p. 210, P.U.F. 1946.

Indeed, to believe that the future is enclosed within eternity is to believe that it already exists in a certain manner and, in other words, that all is already given. All of Bergson's work is directed against such a conception of eternity. His prime intuition is that reality is being invented, being created, and that newness is its most resplendent character, the index of life. The apparent symmetry of past and future arises out of a spatial representation of time which is, in fact, a betrayal of time's true nature.

Bergson's eternity is not closed upon itself, a perfected sum of being. On the contrary, it is open towards the future because it is creative. Eternity creates the real and the possible emerges from it as memory emerges from the present. It is no longer "the conceptual eternity which is an eternity of death, but an eternity of life, a living eternity that is consequently still in motion...." [1] Such an eternity does not exclude time, it is the source of time. "In fact, the more we get used to thinking and perceiving all things *sub specie durationis* the more we enter into real duration. And the deeper we penetrate the more we move in the sense of the principle, transcendent nevertheless, of which we participate, whose eternity must not be an eternity of immutability, but an eternity of life." [2] "God, so defined, is not an unchanging completeness; He is unceasing life, action, and liberty." [3] "Then the Absolute reveals himself very close to us.... He lives with us. Just as we last, so does he, though in certain ways infinitely more concentrated, infinitely less dispersed." [4]

* * *

To biblical thought, as to Bergson, eternity coexists with a creative and inventive time. Here again time is not an unfolding of that which already was in the timeless, in such wise that an eye freed from temporality could see at a glance that which had been given once and for all. Time is truly an endless genesis of "unforeseeable novelty." Eternity therefore could not be beyond time. Time itself must first be accepted for what it really is, before the biblical meaning of eternity can be understood.

The prophet has an understanding of the divine intention in its creative activity. His foreknowledge is restricted in that, as

[1] BERGSON, *La Pensée et le Mouvant*, p. 210, P.U.F. 1946.
[2] BERGSON, *La Pensée et le Mouvant*, p. 176, P.U.F. 1946.
[3] BERGSON, *L'Evolution créatrice*, p. 249, P.U.F. 1946.
[4] BERGSON, *L'Evolution créatrice*, p. 298, P.U.F. 1946.

we have seen, the world is not a moving imitation of some motionless model which might be revealed to him. Precisely for this reason, and because each instant is creation, the prophet cannot tell, for instance, at which precise moment the end will come, except as the farmer knows the coming of harvest by the appearance of the grain.

The biblical dialectic of time and eternity precludes all fatalism and a concept of predestination that would suppose that we are just unwinding a spool of days spun for us in eternity. Neither time nor history would have a sense if they were only the duplication, the progressive copy of an earlier and much more perfect model in which everything has already been given.

This coexistence of time and of eternity expresses the paradox of a creation which is truly inventive and free, and of a self-sufficient Creator who is in need of nothing. For God does not create out of necessity of nature — *ex necessitate divinae naturae* — as He does in the minds of Plotinus and Spinoza. If that were so, there would be no such things as true creation (the real invention of new being), but simply emanation. Time would no longer have any reality. In the couplet "time-eternity" one term would be redundant; time would have to be reabsorbed into eternity through a "conversion."

In biblical metaphysics God creates gratuitously. Time is the creation in process; eternity is the Creators' point of view.

God's creative activity, coexists with His rest (shabbath). We read, on the one hand: "My Father is at work even until now," [1] on the other: "They will not enter into my rest;" [2] and again: "Today have I begotten you." [3] There is a kind of "today" for God — to God a thousand years are as a day — a "today" in which he engenders. But on the seventh day Genesis also says, God "ceased from doing all the work which He had done." [4]

This coexistence of God's self-sufficiency and of His action opens a new perspective and forces on us a hypothesis which the New Testament will confirm: it is through love that God creates.

In this way the biblical dialectic of time and eternity lays the foundation of a metaphysics of liberty for human action and of a theology in which the reason for all things is love.

* * *

---

[1] John 5: 17.
[3] Ps. 2: 7.

[2] Ps. 95: 11.
[4] Gen. 2: 2.

An important corollary concerning human and divine liberty follows from the biblical notion of time.

God created creative beings. History is a work in which divine Action and the action of man cooperate: "We are God's co-workers," *(theou gar esmen sunergoi).* ¹

Human creative action coexists with divine Action; upheld by it, engendered by it, and by it carried forward to the fulness of its autonomy, of its freedom: "I said you are gods." Human action unfolds within divine Action — ("in Him we are, we live and move") — and conversely divine Action works through the activities of man, works through our works without constraining us: "it is God who works in you both will and action," *(Theos gar estin ho energōn en humin kai to thelein kai to energein).* ² God's strength *(dunamis)* works through the action of men: "I am capable of everything in Him Who gives me strength," *(panta ischuō en tō endunamounti me).* *

This graft of a free creative action on the Freedom and Action of the Creator is surely God's master work and the finest paradox of His creation. More than a graft, it is a genesis, the creation of persons drawing their freedom from the spring of all freedom: where the Spirit of the Lord is, there too is freedom.

In this case, clearly, history cannot be something pre-established that man must laboriously unravel. It is instead the unpredictable invention of two separate liberties bound in a common enterprise. Eternity is the sovereignty of uncreated Liberty: "Before the birth of mountains, before You gave birth to earth and world, from eternity to eternity You are, o God. For a thousand years are to Your eyes as the day of yesterday when it passes, and as a watch of the night." ³ "Before Abraham became, I am," *(prin Abraam genesthai egō eimi).* ⁴

The biblical conception of liberty is implied by its conception of time. God created the world, but creation in turn continues to invent itself. Of all creatures man, especially, is the inventor of his own life and destiny. He is a temporal being because he is incomplete and has the power to cooperate in the invention of his destiny. As with the world, so too with individual man, life is not

---

¹ 1 Cor. 3: 9.   ² Phil. 2: 13.
* Phil. 4: 13. Cf. Ephes. 3: 20: the power that works in us; Col. 1: 29: According to his working which works in me mightily; 1 Cor. 12: 6: God works all in all.
³ Ps. 90: 2.   ⁴ John 8: 58.

pre-ordained in an ideal book which his existence must faithfully unfold; it is not a paved road to be followed, but a way to invent. Each man proceeds opening a trail through the brush, creating his path at every step. God's calling does not tell us *what* to do. It drives us out from where we should not be: through failure, boredom, sorrow, we learn which tasks are not for us. God does not, for each act, afford us a model which we would only need to obey faithfully. Instead He commands us to invent, to create a new way, our own. Each of us is like Abraham who "called by God, went forth, knowing not whither." [1]

The metaphysics which deny real time must also deny freedom, simply because they ignore creation, and the power that man has to forge his destiny in collaboration with God. Leibnitz, for instance, says: "The notion of an individual substance once and for all encloses everything that can happen to it. By considering this notion one can see within it all that can ever be truly said of it, just as we can see in the nature of the circle all the properties which can be deduced from it." [2] "The individual notion of Adam encloses everything that will ever happen to him." [3] "When He sees the individual notion or *haeceteitas* of Alexander, God sees in it, simultaneously, the foundation and reason of all the predicates which can be truly asserted of him — (He sees, for instance, that he will conquer Darius and Porus) — to the point of knowing *a priori* (and not from experience), whether he will die a natural death or die by poison..." [4] According to Leibnitz, therefore, the entire destiny of each man is contained within him potentially, implied within his substance, from birth. The potential destiny of each man need only be unfolded, as a symphonic score is unfolded by the orchestra.

Reality can *develop* either by explicitation of what pre-existed entirely, or by organic growth which, by invention of being, brings forth something new. It is in this last manner that the biological germ proceeds. The oak is not in the acorn. To Leibnitz development is a kind of mathematical deduction: a notion which bit by bit reveals its properties and predicates.

Hebrew metaphysics (and Bergsonism), might be called a seminal philosophy, being expressed in terms, not of mathematics, but

[1] Hebr. 11: 8.
[2] LEIBNITZ, *Metaphysical Discourse*, XIII.
[3] LEIBNITZ, *Remarks on the letter of M. Arnaud*, 1686.
[4] LEIBNITZ, *Metaphysical Discourse*, VIII.

of biology.   Against the metaphysics of emanation it maintains that creation endows created beings with creative powers.   It reveals a multitude of creators.   The difficulty here is to understand the relation between the Act of the first Creator and the actions of created creators.

Biblical metaphysics is founded on a dialogue.   If we are to understand it we must stop thinking in terms of a single force and try to penetrate the more complex and much richer play of a world engendered by two freedoms.   The problem of man's free will and God's fore-knowledge, of free will and grace, runs parallel to that of time and of eternity.   We must take care never to install a dichotomy within the common actions of God and man.   "Sic autem ista (grace) cum libero arbitrio operatur, ut tantum illud in primo praeveniat, in caeteris comitetur; ad hoc utique praeveniens, ut jam sibi deinceps cooperetur.   Ita tamen quod a sola gratia coeptum est, pariter ab utroque perficitur: ut mixtim, non singillatim; simul, non vicissim, per singulos profectus operentur.   Non partim gratia, partim liberum arbitrium, sed totum singula opere individuo peragunt.   Totum quidem hoc, et totum illa; sed ut totum in illo, sic totum ex illa." *

---

* St. BERNARD, *Tractatus de gratia et libero arbitrio*, XIV. (Grace), however, operates with free will in such a way that while at first it precedes (free will), subsequently it bears it company.   So grace certainly preceding free will, will thenceforward be cooperating with it.   In this way what is begun by grace alone is completed equally by both of them.   They work jointly, not separately, at the same time, not in turns, through the individual stages.   Grace does not perform one part and free will another; but they accomplish the single act in its entirety through individual working.   The whole, indeed is free will, and the whole is grace; but in such a way that as the whole is in free will, so does the whole proceed from grace.

chapter four

CREATION AND FABRICATION —
THE IDEA OF MATTER

We can get to the significance of the idea of creation only apophatically: it is not man's manner of making, it is not fabrication.

Let us turn again to Bergson for the distinction.... "Fabrication is one thing, organization another. The first is proper to man. It consists in assembling parts of matter shaped so that they may be inserted into one another, to obtain from them a common action. They are, so to speak, assembled around the action which is already their ideal center. Fabrication, therefore, proceeds from periphery to center, or, as the philosopher would put it, from the many to the one. But organization proceeds from the center outwards. It starts from a point which is almost a mathematical point and spreads around it in ever widening waves. Fabrication is more efficient when given a greater quantity of matter. It is a work of concentration and compression. In organization on the contrary there is something explosive: at the outset it needs the least possible space, the minimum of matter. The sperm cell which sets in motion the evolutionary process of embryonic life is one of the smallest cells of the organism; even then it is only a small fraction of the semen which actually participates in the operation." ★ ★

Fabrication must start from some "matter." It takes a pre-existing multiplicity and orders it to an end. The act of creation on the contrary does not proceed from any matter, from something given in scatteredness. It unfolds from a unity which grows with the assimilation of outer elements. "A glance at embryonic

---

★ Cf. note p. 17.
★ ★ BERGSON, *L'Evolution créatrice*, p. 93; for a criticism of the idea of fabrication see, *Plotinus*, Enn. 5: 8, 7.

development" shows "that life proceeds quite differently (from the human worker assembling parts). Life does not proceed by association and addition of elements but by dissociation and multiplication." [1]

In fabrication therefore the many is a beginning. It must be bound by a *sundesmos* which still cannot make of it a real (that is, an organic) unity. In created organic reality the many is to be found only at the end, in death: it is the dust of decay.

Fabrication works on something which is already created. It does not take into account the originality or the peculiar structure of the element on which it works unless this structure is important in relation to the end which the workman has in mind. That is what we mean when we call the given element "matter." "Fabrication works exclusively on raw matter. We mean that even if it uses organized materials it treats them like inert objects without any concern for the life which shaped them." [2]

The fabricated object has its own ontological status. [*] As such it is not a substance. It is a natural element which fulfills a function, plays the role of chair, weapon, or tool. But mere function cannot confer the title of substance. To the innocent observer who does not know its use, the object appears as a peculiar arrangement of its elements. To this observer a chair is simply a disfigured tree. There is no chair substance, only wood, serving as a chair. What exists in the fabricated object is the natural element, wood, metal, etc. In other words, what *exists* is that which is *created*.

* * *

Idolatry is a tendency to fabricate a god. It is therefore a refusal of God's transcendence: "Come, make a god for us who will walk before us." [3]

The idol is a fabricated object, *maase iad haadam*, "a work of the hands of man," which is mistaken for a being, for something created, much more, for a god. Of course, the fabricated object is not even a being. The only thing real about it, the only thing about it that *exists* is the created element that has been worked and molded. "Idols are silver and gold, works of the hands of man.

---

[1] BERGSON, *L'Evolution créatrice*, p. 90, P.U.F. 1946.
[2] BERGSON, *L'Evolution créatrice*, p. 154, P.U.F. 1946.
[*] Cf. ARISTOTLE, *Phys.* II, 1, 192 b.
[3] Ex. 32: 1.

They have a mouth but do not speak." [1] "Woe to him who says unto wood: 'arise'; 'awake' to speechless stone. Will it instruct?... See it is covered in gold and silver, there is no breath of life within it." [2] "They drank wine and praised gods of gold and silver, brass, iron, wood, and stone..." [3] "...which neither see nor hear and which know nothing." [4] "There you will serve gods which are works of the hands of man, wood and stone, which do not see, nor hear, nor feel." [5] "You have seen their abominations and their idols, wood and stone, silver and gold." [6]   The texts on this subject are numberless.

Idolatry is first of all an ontological error, a mistake concerning being.   When mind turns to an idol and mistakes it for a being, it is misled, for it reaches only a natural created element, wood, metal, etc.   The being sought after is lacking because fabrication is not creation.   "Provoke me not to anger with the work of your hands." [7]   The being, the god that is sought in the idol is not there.   Idolatry reaches for emptiness: "Every craftsman is ashamed of his idol, because his molten image is but a lie; there is no breath in it, it is an emptiness, a work of trickery." [8]   Idolatry is an ontological deception.   "You will no longer adore the work of your hands." [9]   "We shall no longer say 'our god' to the work of our hands." [10]   The Bible often calls idols *nothingnesses, emptinesses, elilim.* [11]

But the fabrication of idols does not necessarily have recourse to sensible materials.   There is an inner fabrication, a secret industry of idols.   "Cursed be the man who makes a carved image or a molten image, abomination to Yhwh, a work of a craftsman's hands, and who places it in a secret place." [12]   This secret place can be what the Bible calls "the secret of the heart."   "These people have raised upon their hearts infamous idols." [13]   "Whosoever in the houses of Israel or among the foreigners living in Israel turns himself from me, raises his infamous idols in his heart." [14]   The practice of idolatry and withdrawal from Yhwh are a single movement, a turning to non-being, because Yhwh is *Who Is,*

---

[1] Ps. 115: 4.
[2] Hab. 2: 19.
[3] Dan. 5: 4.
[4] Dan. 5: 23.
[5] Deut. 4: 28.
[6] Deut. 29: 17.
[7] Jer. 25: 6-7; 32: 30; 44: 8.
[8] Jer. 10: 14.
[9] Mic. 5: 13.
[10] Hos. 14: 3.
[11] Lev. 26: 1; 1 Is. 2: 8; 10: 10; Ps. 96: 5.
[12] Deut. 27: 15.
[13] Ez. 14: 3.
[14] Ez. 14: 7.

whereas the idol is nothing. "We know that there are no idols in the world." [1]

We therefore find in the Bible a dialectic of being and nothingness. But here nothingness does not precede being, it is not the underlying reality, the original reality recovered and surmounted by being. In the Bible being is the first thing: *"in the beginning* Elohim..." [2]

The dialectic between being and nothingness is, in practice, the choice between *Who Is* and the nonentity of the idol. Nonentity has no reality in itself, it is the experience of the man who moves away from God, who flees God. Idolatry is a choice which separates us from the Being and joins us with nonentity. Conversely a return to Yhwh is first of all the abandonment, the rejection of all idols.

The war against idolatry into which we are drawn by the prophets of Israel reveals to us an ontology in daily life. Idolatry is primarily a confusion of the fabricated object with the created being. It is also a confusion, more difficult to overcome, of the created and the Creator. Only the idea that the whole universe is created, (an idea which implies the transcendence of the Creator, "the God Who made the world and all it contains") [3] can overcome this confusion. All sensible things are creatures, *natura naturata*. Astrolatry, for instance, is a confusion of creature and creator. "They have foresaken divine truth in favor of falsehood, they have adored and served the creature instead of the Creator." [4]

"Because you did not see a shape on the day that Yhwh spoke to you from the midst of the fire on Horeb, take care of your soul lest you pervert yourselves and make some carved image, figure of some idol, likeness of man or woman, likeness of a bird which flies in the heaven, likeness of a beast which crawls on the ground, likeness of a fish which lives in the waters beneath the earth. Therefore take care lest, lifting your eyes to heaven and seeing the sun, the moon and the stars, the host of heaven, you feel moved to fall down and worship them." [5]

* * *

---

[1] 1 Cor. 8: 4.
[3] Acts 17: 24.
[5] Deut. 4: 15-19.
[2] Gen. 1: 1.
[4] Rom. 1: 25.

The idea of matter may sometimes be an obstacle to a correct understanding of the creative act. If we think that "matter" underlies reality we are once again confusing fabrication and creation, for we assume that reality was hewn out of a preexisting element just like some object of our workmanship.

The body does not model itself on the corpse. An organism is not the synthesis of multiplicity made one by some principle of unity called the soul. The organism grows from a germ which is a unity, and spreads outwards by assimilating exterior elements and integrating them. To say that a living organism is a composite of multiple matter unified by a "form" is an inversion of understanding, an assumption that the multiple came first, that life is constructed from its ashes.

Fabrication, we have said, assembles various materials and binds them together within a certain form. This form, however, remains outward, extrinsic, and does not really "inform" the material used. Hence a dualism of "matter" and "form." Creative organization, contrariwise, actually does shape the elements which it incorporates; once taken in they are no longer what they were nor what they will return to after death. Unity rules, not outwardly, but inwardly by transformation. The whole precedes the parts because a living organism *is* a form and man *is* a "living soul." With life there is not substantial duality of "matter" and "form."

Fabrication gives a useful shape to an organic element which we call material or matter. Since the original structure of this element *in se* is of no particular interest to us, except in relation to the object we are building, we tend to say that the material has no form. Of course this is just a manner of speech; wood has a form, a structure infinitely more complex and subtle than any we could ever give it; right down to the molecular and atomic levels, wood is a form. But since it is not the form we choose to give it, table, divinity, or skiff, we call the element which we use formless.

If we imagine that the world was fabricated as by human craft, we will be forced to give chronological priority, in the visible world, to an original "matter," a formless, orderless reality to which a demiurge later added a form, an order which is that of the cosmos. Matter, we will have to say, is disorder, formlessness, indeterminacy, which must be ordered, shaped, and determined. Beneath reality, it will then seem, there lies a primeval lack of order which had to be overcome. "(Anaxagoras) recognizes as principles the One (which is simple and unmixed), and the Other, just as we Platonists suppose the Indeterminate *(to aoriston)* to precede any kind of determination or participation in some form." [1]

It seems that the negative ideas of *chaos*, *chōra* and *apeiron* play an important part in the genesis of the idea of "matter." *

* * *

Bergson has attempted to analyse the unconscious roots of these negative ideas, disorder and nothingness. His criticism touches on two points:

(1) "When the philosopher speaks of chaos he is mere transporting to the speculative level two ideas (which are thus raised to an absolute and hence emptied of all meaning and effective content) that were designed for practical application, and therefore refer to a specific kind of matter and order but not to all order nor to all matter." [2]   For "the idea of disorder has definite meaning in the field of human industry or manufacture, but not in that of creation". [3]   And when we speak of nonentity, he adds, it is because our mind, "accustomed to assembling parts in a relative void, imagines that the real fills I know not what absolute void." [4]

(2) "We feel that a divinely creative will or mind is too full of itself in its enormous reality to allow the idea of a lack of order or a lack of being even to touch it. To imagine the possibility of an absolute disorder, and *a fortiori*, of nothingness would amount to admitting that this will or mind might not have been at all, and that would be a weakness incompatible with its nature which is strength." [5]

"If order did not seem to us a conquest over something or an addition to something (in this case an absence of order) the realism of antiquity would not have spoken of a "matter" to which the Idea is joined, nor would modern idealism have supposed a "sensible diversity" that understanding organizes into nature." [6]

---

[1] ARISTOTLE, *Met.* 989 b, 18.
* Cf. A. RIVAUD, *Le problème du devenir et la notion de matière dans la philosophie grecque depuis les origines jusqu'à Théophraste,* 1906.
[2] BERGSON, *La Pensée et le Mouvant,* p. 68, P.U.F. 1946.
[3] BERGSON, *La Pensée et le Mouvant,* p. 108, P.U.F. 1946.
[4] BERGSON, *La Pensée et le Mouvant,* p. 105, P.U.F. 1946.
[5] BERGSON, *La Pensée et le Mouvant,* p. 66, P.U.F. 1946.
[6] BERGSON, *L'Evolution créatrice,* p. 233, P.U.F. 1946.

"At the bottom of all ancient philosophy there necessarily lies this postulate: there is more in the motionless than in the moving, and it is by diminution or attenuation that the passage is made from immutability to becoming."

"So, in order to provoke change, something negative, at most a zero, must be added to the Ideas.   This (negative something) is the Platonic 'non-entity' and the Aristotelian 'matter' — a metaphysical zero which, set beside the idea like the arithmetical zero beside the unit, multiplies it in space and time. The motionless and simple idea is refracted by it in an indefinitely propagated movement.   By right there should only be the immutable Ideas, immutably locked into one another.   In fact, matter superadds its void to them, thereby launching universal becoming.   Matter, slipping between the ideas, is the intangible nothingness which, like a suspicion come between two loving hearts, causes the endless agitation, the eternal inquietude." [1]

* * *

If the idea of matter seems ruled by confusion it is because in this term there meet at least three different views:

(1) a dualism, of Platonic and Orphic origin, later picked up by Plotinus and rationalized by Descartes.   In this current of thought matter itself is a substance, *res extensa*, which stands opposed to mind, *res cogitans*.   Without a doubt affective currents of a Manichean kind flow into this dualist conception of matter against which Berkeley's protest was directed.

(2) the Aristotelian and Thomist metaphysics, to which, in principle at least, matter is not a thing, a substance, but a metaphysical aspect of reality.   "In this sense there is no matter *qua* matter.   But such or such a factor *is matter* in relation to such or such a form." [2]   "The conception of matter is relative; for

---

[1] BERGSON, *L'Evolution Créatrice*, p. 316, P.U.F. 1946. Bergson does not really profess this criticism of the idea of matter which is implied in the criticism of the ideas of not-being and of disorder, and which we discover in these texts. On the contrary, Bergson professes dualism.   On the subject of the part of "matter," "materiality" and in general the movement of inversion in the Bergsonian cosmogony, cf. Appendix I, The Neo-Platonism of Bergson.

[2] LALANDE, *Voc. Phil.* s.v.

different matter is suited to different forms." *   "Materia et forma dicuntur relative ad invicem." **   Matter here is not a physical concept nor a physical substance.   It is a metaphysical structure of concrete reality.   Dualism on the contrary considers "matter" and "body" to be physical concepts, empirical facts.

(3) Modern science, which speaks the language of Descartes but is finding more and more that matter has properties quite contrary to those which Descartes attributed to it: energy, for instance.   Modern science gives the name of matter to what Aristotle called the sensible.   This to Aristotle was composed of "matter" and "form" in a quite different sense.

*   *
*

These analyses had to be made in order to distinguish the ideas of creation and fabrication, and in order to define more clearly the Hebrew conception of the sensible in so far as it differs from the Greek: *the biblical world is a world in which the idea of "matter" does not occur.*   This is its characteristic — a negative one — in contrast to Greek thought, in which the idea of matter, and the dualism, "matter-form" played so great a role.

Hebrew is a very concrete language.   It has words only for what exists.   It has no word for "matter" nor for "body" because these concepts do not cover any empirical realities.   Nobody ever saw any "matter," nor a "body," such as they are defined by substantial dualism.   The sensible elements, wood, iron, water, are not "matter;" they are sensible realities, which in Aristotle's metaphysics

---

* *Phys.* 2, 2, 194 b, 8.   From the point of view of knowledge, matter being but a relative can no more be known in itself than it can exist by itself.   One could not point it out and say: "That is matter."   O. HAMELIN, *Le Système d'Aristote*, 1931, p. 266.   Cf. ARISTOTLE, *Physics* I, 191 : "The subject nature can be known by analogy.   For the relationship of bronze to statue, of wood to bed, or in general of formless matter to whatever has a form, such is the relationship of matter to substance, to the particular individual, to being."   Note that the examples used by Aristotle are all taken from the field of *fabrication*.   It remains to be seen whether the analogy is still valid between what occurs in the field of fabrication and what occurs in the field of creation.   The idea of *shapeless matter* merits the criticism that Bergson applies to the ideas of *disorder* and *not-being*: it is a pseudo-idea that arises out of a confusion between two orders, the order of human fabrication and the order of being.   While the idea of matter is valid in the utilitarian language of industry, it has no ontological significance in the order of natural organic reality.

** "Matter and form are said to be relative to one another."   St. THOMAS, *de Princ. Nat.*

are abstractly dissected into two principles: matter and form.   If we wish to refer to the sensible as "matter," there can be no objection.   It is just a question of words.   But then we must make quite sure of our meaning and not refer to the sensible world the characteristics attributed by dualism, and in fact by Manicheism, to their own peculiar myth of an inconceivable "matter substance."

Precisely because it is not dualist, Hebrew, more than any other language, has an understanding, a love of the elements and of the flesh.

It would be a great mistake to think of Hebrew thought as a form of idealism.   It is quite the contrary.   It dispenses only with the dualism which calls upon two principles of being to explain the sensible world.

Indeed Hebrew thought is as far away from what we call idealism as it is from what we call materialism.   More correctly, it transcends the dichotomy which brought about these two antinomic systems, both of which rest on the same postulate: a dualism.

Hebrew thought resembles idealism in its belief that the sensible world is intelligible, that the world is essentially porous to intelligence because it is created by the word.

But at the same time Hebrew thought is irreconcilably opposed to idealism by its realistic metaphysics of being, its love of the carnal, * and its conception of work and action in the elements. It is the thought of shepherds and farmers.

And in this sense it would resemble materialism.   Its rejection of dualism gives an importance to the sensible and the corporeal which calls to mind the physics of the Stoics.   But against a materialism such as that of the 19th century it maintains its conception of the intelligibility of the bodily, and its refusal of any Manichean entity, the idea of an anti-spiritual matter, which would be characterized by an opaqueness to the spirit.

One might call Hebrew thought a poetic materialism or a carnal idealism.

* * *

In Hebrew thought, we have seen, there is no idea of matter. Neither is it troubled with the Hellenic and Western concepts of non-entity and disorder, so familiar to us.

---

* "Carnal" here means" incarnational"; it has no reference to the lusts of the flesh.

"We proceed from absence to presence, from void to fulness, as a result of the fundamental illusion of our understanding," Bergson writes. [1] The concept of nothingness he adds, "is often the hidden spring, the invisible motor of philosophic thought." "Existence seems to me a conquest over nothingness. I imagine that there might not, indeed, that there should not be anything, and I am surprised then to see that something is." [*] The same holds true of the idea of disorder. "There might not be any order at all. The mathematical order of things being a conquest over disorder..." [2] "...it would seem that disorder would be first by rights." [3]

It is characteristic of Hebrew thought, as opposed to Greek and Western thought, that it is not troubled by negative ideas of nothingness and disorder. Hebrew thought is not haunted by the idea of an original void that should be there "by rights" and that has to be overcome, or of a disorder, a chaos, that has to be mastered, because its threatening presence might undermine reality. In the beginning stands, not void, but Him whose name is: "I am," Yhwh, the living God Who created heaven and earth. "*In the beginning*, God..."

No original void preceeds being because it is written that God, the essential Being, exists from all eternity; disorder is not primeval because the Hebrew mind does not conceive an indeterminate disorganized matter underlying the determination of form; there is no "matter", no "body" apart from a soul, for living beings *are* living souls.

There are indeed texts in the Bible that speak of a disorder, a chaos overcome by God. For instance: "In the beginning God created heaven and earth. Earth was empty and void. Darkness

---

[1] BERGSON, *L'Evolution créatrice*, p. 275, P.U.F. 1946.
[*] Bergson's criticism of the idea of not-being is in a certain sense the argument of St. Anselm in reverse. *At least one being* is necessary. We are backed up to being. Likewise in the biblical universe the idea of absolute not-being has no meaning. Concerning the idea of not-being, cf. PLOTINUS, *Enn.* 6, 8. "It seems that, if we imagine some difficulties concerning the nature (of the One) it is because we first conceive a space or place similar to the chaos of the poets, and then introduce the First into this place, this space that is born or that exists in our imagination, having done this we inquire whence he came and how he came here; we inquire about his presence and his existence as though he were a foreign being." *Ibid.*, p. 276.
[2] BERGSON, *L'Evolution créatrice*, p. 221, P.U.F. 1946.
[3] BERGSON, *L'Evolution créatrice*, p. 232, P.U.F. 1946.

covered the deep." [1] Yet these ideas of a chaos, of an invading sea, of a dragon which God restrained [2] do not play the same part in the biblical conception of being as do the ideas of chaos and indeterminacy in the mind of the Greek philosophers. God is the Creator of all that exists. There could not have been an original coexistence between Him and an uncreated, primeval disorder. There was no strife between God and a Chaos, conceived as anti-God. The world was not fabricated with some sort of primitive matter, starting with a chaos which had to be fashioned into a cosmos. In Genesis we read, first, that God created heaven and earth; then that the earth was *tohu wabohu*, chaotic; but this is simply because God had not yet made it inhabitable. [3] Disorder *follows* reality, does not *precede* it. *

We should add that these references to a primitive chaos, often personified, are found especially among the later poets. They are not found in any ancient narrative such as the Yahwist narrative of creation. Also a careful comparison of the first chapter of Genesis with the Babylonian Cosmogony of *Enuma Elish* proves that biblical thought, because it rejects all theogony and *a fortiori* any form of "theomachy," categorically refuses to see in the act of creation any real battle between God and chaos.

---

[1] Gen. 1: 2.
[2] Cf. Is. 27: 1; Job 38: 8; Ps. 74: 13.
[3] Cf. Is. 45: 18.
* Contrariwise Hesiodus: "First among beings was Chaos, and next came Earth., the great womb of Earth."

chapter five

THE SENSIBLE

Hebrew thought is unhampered by the dualist concept of "matter." Consequently the sensible world gains an importance and fulfills a function in it which it never held in Greek thought. For in Greek thought the idea of matter covered the world with a cloud of unintelligibility. It is the idea of matter which reveals the latent Manicheism of Greek philosophy.

In the world of the Bible the sensible is not deprived of meaning. It is not necessary to add to it, from without, a meaning which it does not contain in its very nature. One need only free the sensible on the one hand from a dualism which reduces it to the state of an "indeterminate" reality *(apeiron)*, and on the other hand from a certain conception of becoming, of the multiple and of bodily existence.

The Hebrew loves the sensible world simply because he is not a dualist. He has a sense, an understanding of the elemental because he does not by definition condemn the sensible to be divided from, and *other* than, the intelligible. To him the sensible is neither bad nor sinful. Matter is not the root of evil; the world is "very good." The Hebrew understands the carnal because he discerns the spiritual sap which courses through it. The biblical world unfolds before us the exact opposite of the Manichean world. Understanding of the carnal, love of the elemental, understanding and love of contemplation and the spiritual are all one from the Hebrew point of view. They are one because the sensible world is a language: it was created by the word.

* * *

The world was created by the word. "God said: let there be light! and there was light.... God said: let there be a firmament

between the waters... let there be luminaries.... God said: let
the waters swarm with a multitude of living beings.... God said:
let the land produce living beings...." [1]

"By the word of Yhwh the heavens were made, and by the breath
of His mouth all His army... For He spoke, and all was made.
He commanded and all existed." [2]

"In the beginning was the Word (Memra, in Hebrew). All
was made by Him, and without Him nothing was made of that
which was made." [3]

"By faith we do recognize that the world was formed by the
word of God in such a way that the things which we see were
not made from visible things." [4]

We have here a constant theme in the tradition of biblical and
post-biblical Jewish thought even up to the Cabala and Hassidism.
It excludes any kind of substantial dualism. What we Westerners
call "matter" was also created by the word. All sensible realities,
all nature, have their principle in a word. For this reason they
are essentially intelligible. Because we are used to Cartesian
dualism we tend to think of matter as of something entirely inert.
To the Cabala on the contrary, matter is animated, it is, in the words
of Novalis, a petrification of God. The least particle of matter
contains enormous quantities of concentrated and dormant energy.
The speculations of the alchemists and the metaphysics of Leibnitz
are founded on this dynamistic conception of matter, just the
contrary of that professed by Descartes, and which Spinoza
and Leibnitz reject. *

---

[1] Gen. I.   [2] Ps. 33: 6.
[3] John I: I.   [4] Hebr. II: 3.
* The Cabala rejects the idea of creation but keeps the biblical tradition according
to which the word is origin of the sensible world. The Cabala's Pantheism and
its doctrine of the word cause it to reject the idea of "matter" in a dualist sense:
"Fundamenta Philosophiae... quae omnem Creationem proprie dictam negat,
Essentiamque supponit Divinam quasi Corporeo-Spiritualem, Mundumque
Materialem aliquo modo Spiritum" (Kabbala denudata, t. I, pars IIa, p. 293).
"Ex nihilo nihil posse creari." Hence: "nec materiam creari posse" (ibid.) and
"Nullam igitur Materiam esse in rerum natura." "Quidquid vero est, Spiritum
esse." All sensible realities, which we call material, are parts of the divine
Essence. "Ex contractis his partibus constare mundum qui vocatur Materialem,
cum revera adhuc Spiritualis sit, constans utique ex divisis Spiritibus, parti-
culisve Divinae essentiae, in Monadas Punctave Physica contractis et constipatis.
Contractionem hanc esse statum somni seu Soporis." (Ibid.) Matter is a
"coalitio monadum spiritualium torpentium." (K.D. I, 6, p. 310). No need
to stress the analogy with the metaphysics of Leibnitz. J. G. WACHTER, in a

Because it was created by a word the sensible is meaningful. It is itself a language, the substantial manifestation of a creative word.

But this word is spoken *to* someone. There is no word in solitude. The world is a word because there was foreseen a hearer to hear it, a mind to discern its purport beneath the sensible appearance, a tongue to answer it. Creation by the word implies a dialogue. The world is a work of revelation waiting to be grasped by understanding; man's attention is demanded to draw from it the intelligible content, elaborate it for his sustenance and his delight; man's answer is demanded to name the truth, name, praise and rehearse the spiritual teaching of the subsistent carnal writ. "And Yhwh God formed from the earth all the animals of the fields and all the birds of the sky. And He made them go towards man to see what he would cry to them. And whatsoever man cried to them, to every living soul, that is its name." [1]

All things sensible are meaningful and all creation is a discourse in which the elements appear as a consistent and subsisting vocabulary. Every biblical writer from Genesis to the Apocalypse uses the same symbolic lexicon with a remarkable consistency. All speak the same elemental language, the same syntax binds the terms, the same grammar allows them to function without releasing the meaning from its roots.

Through the mediation of the elements there is a "cosmic" circulation from God to man, from man to God. "As rain and

---

work which incidentally was read and carefully annotated by Leibnitz, *Elucidarius Cabalisticus*, Rome 1706, compared the metaphysics of the Cabala with that of Spinoza. Wachter notes that in Cabala as in Spinoza there is no creation. "Ex hoc deinde Principio varias conclusiones parturiunt Cabalei, utpote Materiam nec creari, nec ob vilitatem essentiae suae a se existere posse, proinde nec ullam esse in universo materiam, vel spiritum et materiam unum idemque esse... In quibus omnibus consentientem secum habent Spinozam..." (p. 45). One can better understand the opposition of Spinoza and Leibnitz to Cartesian dualism and to the purely mechanical Cartesian conception of matter. "Hinc saepe monet (sc. Spinoza, Epist. 73) a Cartesio materiam male definiri par extensionem" (p. 46). "Nulla igitur juxta Spinozam in universo Materia est, sed quidquid est, res funditus praestantissima est, id est, uti Cabalei vocant, Spiritus..." (p. 46). This rejection of the idea of inert "matter" allows all sensible reality to be considered animated. "Deum produxisse mundum vividum et animatum, recepta cabaleorum doctrina est... Nam cum nulla, uti tradunt, in universo materia sit, mors utique nulla est, sed omnia utcunque videantur mortua, erunt diversis gradibus animata." Cf. SPINOZA, *Eth*. II, schol. propr. XIII "Omnia quamvis diversis gradibus animata tamen sunt."

[1] Gen. 2: 19.

snow fall from the sky and return not to it before they have watered and fecundated the earth, before they have made it germinate, before they have given seed to the sower and bread to the man who eats; so it is with My word that goes forth from My mouth and does not return to Me without effect, for it performs what I have willed and accomplishes that wherefore I sent it." [1] "I shall betroth you to Me forever... and you will know Yhwh. And in that day it will happen, — word of Yhwh, — I shall answer to the heavens and they will answer to earth; earth will answer to the wheat and the new wine and the oil, and they to Jezrahel." [2]

In the marriage of Yhwh and Israel the elements are the words of a dialogue of gift and oblation. There is some analogy, in the communion they afford, to the savor of the communion of human lovers.

"He made her go up on the heights of the land, and Israel has eaten the produce of the fields; He gave her to suck the honey of the rock, the oil which comes from the hardest rock, cream of the cow and milk of ewe with the fat of lambs... with the flour of wheat, and you have drunk the blood of the vine, the frothy wine. But... you have despised the rock of your salvation... you have abandoned the rock which engendered you, and forgotten the God who bore you." [3]   "Yhwh answered and said to His people: behold I shall send to you wheat, new wine and oil, and you will be satiated." [4] "She has not recognized that it is I Who gave her the grain, the new wine and the oil, and I Who multiplied the silver and the gold... therefore shall I take back my grain in its time and My new wine in its season." [5] "They will come with cries of joy to the heights of Zion; they will crowd toward the gifts of Yhwh, towards the wheat, towards the new wine, towards the oil... their soul will be like a watered garden." [6] "He has given to them the wheat of heaven." [7]

***

* * *

If throughout the books of the Bible we follow the references to elements, water, oil and wine, wheat and bread, the stone, the

---

[1] Is. 55: 10-11.

[2] Hos. 2: 21-24.

[3] Deut. 32: 13-17.

[4] Joel 2: 19.

[5] Hos. 2: 10-11.

[6] Jer. 31: 12.

[7] Ps. 78: 24.

rock, dust (which is, we saw, the image of death), we can uncover their perennial meaning, their symbolism.

Between rain and the word of God there appeared to the Hebrews an analogy. By its geographical situation Palestine is entirely dependent upon rain. Out of this material disadvantage a spiritual advantage arises: Israel cannot retire into itself in self-sufficiency. It depends on rain, on the word of Yhwh. It depends as does a lover who is glad not to be able to do without his beloved. Israel is materially in that uncertainty which makes it totally depend upon the love of Yhwh; the dialogue cannot be interrupted, under pain of death. The gratuity of rain recalls the gratuity of the word. "Yhwh will come to us like a shower, like a late rain watering the earth." [1]

From Genesis to Revelation, beginning with Melchizedek, king of Salem, who brought bread and wine to Abraham, [2] vine and wine, bread and wheat hold a mystical significance.

Israel is called a vine: "The vine of Yhwh of hosts, that is the house of Israel." [3]

Wine, the yearly vintage, depends upon the gift of rain ("I shall command the clouds to let rain fall upon her no longer"), [4] for wine "which rejoices the heart of man" is a figure of the spirit, of the spiritual life which is love. "Let him kiss me with a kiss of his mouth, for your love is better than wine" says the Beloved in the Song of Songs. [5] We find this same meaning in the New Testament where the renewal of the spiritual life is compared to new wine which should not be put into old wine-skins. [6] Surely it is significant that one of the first "signs" of Jesus was the turning of water to wine at Cana, at a wedding. It is in that same understanding that we must read the cry of the Apocalypse: "Harm not the oil and the wine." [7]

Oil must also stand for something spiritual. It is the sacrament which anointed kings in Israel. From this anointment they received gifts of strength and understanding. In the words of the Psalmist the Messiah is one anointed with an oil of "rejoicing." "Your name is an oil poured forth." [8] Joel's proclamation ("Yhwh answered and said to His people: behold I shall send you wheat,

[1] Hos. 6: 3.
[2] Gen. 14: 18.
[3] Is. 5: 7.
[4] Is. 5: 6.
[5] Song of Songs 1: 2.
[6] Matth. 9: 17; Mark 2: 22; Luke 5: 37.
[7] Apoc. 6: 6.
[8] Song of Songs 1: 3.

new wine and oil") foretells a profusion of the spirit: "I shall pour forth My spirit on all flesh."

The meaning of perfume in the liturgy of the Old Testament is linked to this significance of oil. Perfume and incense bind oil with fire: "Let my prayer be before your face like incense and the lifting of my hands like an evening offering." [1]

Bread and wheat are of prime importance in the Old Testament as in the New. The consecration of the eucharistic bread and wine effected in the New Testament (symbolizing the shedding of blood), had a long preparation through all of the Old Testament. It is this long tradition which allows Christ's hearers to give the fullest sense to His words: "I am the living bread," [2] "I am the bread of life." [3] The analogy with manna is also pointed out. [4] The Christian sacraments cannot be understood apart from the history which ripened their significance. In a dualist metaphysics they remain unintelligible.

The elements created by the word are meaningful. Bread and wine give joy and sustenance. When the Word Himself comes in the flesh He consecrates the bread and the wine, teaching that He is the "true" bread, [5] that He *is* food and that His gift is the food which will bring life to His creatures. The wine tells us that love shed His blood "for His friends." The bread stands for the essential food.

The offering of the host is man's answer in the material dialogue. The eating of it becomes an understanding of the mystery, an understanding which allows us to discern the truly present Word beneath the visible sign.

What is the meaning of salt? It is the love of man, and the charity that he brings with his offering: "Whatever you bring in offering will be salted; you will not allow the salt of the alliance with your God to be lacking in your offering; on all your offerings you will offer salt." [6] Perfume for incense will also be: "salted pure and holy." [7] God proclaims an "alliance of salt." [8] And Christ preaches: "Every man will be salted with fire." [9]

Fire in the Bible is the sign of God's love, His jealousy and His wrath. "Yhwh your God is a devouring fire, a jealous God." [10]

---

[1] Ps. 141: 2.
[3] John 6: 35.
[5] John 6: 32.
[7] Exod. 30: 35.
[9] Mark 9: 49.

[2] John 6: 51.
[4] John 6: 32.
[6] Lev. 2: 13.
[8] Num. 18: 19.
[10] Deut. 4: 24.

It is fire which purifies, destroying the imperfect, perfecting the gold. "The Light of Israel will be a fire and her Holy One a flame to consume and to devour her thorns and brambles in a single day." [1] "The whole world will be devoured by the fire of My jealousy." [2] The love of Yhwh is demanding because Yhwh is a strong God, a living God. Fire is His sign, fire which destroys the corruptible and leaves only the incorruptible. God appears surrounded by fire: "Yhwh speaks from the midst of fire." [3] "For of all flesh, who has heard, as we have, the voice of the living God speaking from the midst of fire, and lived." [4] Fire again is the sign, the criterion invoked by Elias: "The god who answers by fire, that one is God." [5]

Fire is an ambiguous power, both kind and awful. So too the love of God, the delight of the already purified saint, is a torment to any man who experiences it without communing with it. It is this man, persecuted by God's love, who cries: "What is there between Thyself and myself?" This love is implacably exigent: "Love is strong as death, jealousy is unyielding as hell itself." [6] "If you foresake Yhwh to serve foreign gods He will consume you." [7] "They brought before Yhwh a foreign fire which they had not been told to bring. Then a fire went forth from Yhwh and devoured them and they died before Yhwh." [8] "The wrath and jealousy of Yhwh will flare up." [9] The same symbolism is found in the preaching of John the Baptist: "He will baptize you with the Holy Ghost and with fire. The fan is in His hand, and very thoroughly He will clear His threshing floor — the wheat He will collect into the granary and the chaff He will burn with a fire that cannot be put out." [10]

To endure the love of the living God a *habitus* is necessary, which allows man, instead of dying, to live and to partake of the life of this fire, the terror of Israel. This *habitus* will be given by fire itself: "Every man will be salted with fire." [11] It was Christ's mission to light this regenerating fire of life designed to destroy whatever cannot partake of incorruptible life: "I have come to cast a fire upon the earth, and what better wish can I have than that it should be kindled?" [12]

---

[1] Is. 10: 17.
[2] Soph. 3: 8.
[3] Deut. 4: 12: 15, 33; 5: 21.
[4] Deut. 5: 23.
[5] I Kings 18: 24.
[6] Song of Songs 8: 16.
[7] Jos. 24: 19.
[8] Lev. 10: 1: 2.
[9] Deut. 29: 19.
[10] Matth. 3: 11.
[11] Mark 9: 49.
[12] Luke 12: 49.

And the Holy Ghost, descending upon the disciples shows Himself by "tongues of fire." [1]

When the New Testament says that "God is love" it reveals the same truth as did the Old when it spoke of the Lord as a fire. The Epistle to the Hebrews says: "It is a terrible thing to fall into the hands of the living God."

It is this same symbolic language that is still spoken by liturgy, with fire as with the other elements: "Accendat in nobis Dominus ignem sui amoris, et flammam aeternae caritatis." "Let God kindle in us the fire of his love, and the flame of eternal Charity."

* * *

To a lover of the Bible the most fascinating thing in Plato's universe is the doctrine of participation. The sensible refers us to an intelligible world, of which it is an image and from which it proceeds. Beauty is participation. * Therefore beauty is knowledge. Sensible realities are signs which, by an ascending dialectic, lead us to contemplation. It is through its sense of contemplation that Platonism is akin to the biblical tradition.

They differ nonetheless, and differ on the amount of ontological consistency, the amount of being, which they grant to sensible reality. For the sensible does not have the same ontological status in the two metaphysical world-views.

In Platonism the sensible is a reflection, a shadow of the intelligible; it participates in the Idea through degradation. To join the Idea we must "flee" this nether region.

Now in the biblical world the sensible participates in the intelligible by the fact of creation. It is in itself not only an image but also a subsisting reality. It is both being and sign. Here lies the originality of the biblical point of view. The sensible and the concrete have in it a greater consistency, a greater ontological reality, than they have in Platonism, yet they are in no way less significant. On the contrary, it is by granting to the sensible its whole existential consistency that biblical tradition uncovers

---

[1] Acts 11, 3.

* Cf. PLOTINUS, *Enn.* 1: 6, 1: "Some beings like bodies are beautiful, not because of their substance, but through participation *(methezei)*."

its treasures of intelligibility and significance. Words which exist: such is, in the biblical universe, the paradoxical definition of sensible realities.

In Platonism it appears necessary to diminish and extenuate reality and the consistency of the sensible in order to allow it to become a sign of the world of Ideas. The sensible must be evanescent in order to play its role as an image. Biblical thought, however, maintains both aspects, ontological reality and significance.

How can things be, at the same time, both real and significant? Human signs and images that are of our own making, are never subsisting beings, they are essentially unreal. It is perhaps for this reason that we find it so hard to conceive that a sign can be an existing reality and that a being can signify.

It should be noted that Christian philosophers, like St. Thomas or St. Bonaventure, who make the Platonic doctrine of participation part of their own thoughts, correct it with a realistic ontology, that of Aristotle.

* * *

In this context we may ask: what is the difference between the parable *(mashal)* and the symbol of the Platonist?

The *mashal* is either a sensible material fact or a historical event which signifies some invisible reality. The meaning is contained *in* the signifying fact, *in* the concrete reality. We do not have to flee the sensible in order to reach the intelligible. The teller of parables invites us to discern a meaning not affixed to the fact from without, but actually immanent in it, a constituent part of the fact.

In the myth of the cave Plato says that to know the intelligible we must get out, turn away from the sensible which is but a shadow. The Platonic symbol, to represent a metaphysical or theological reality, has recourse to myth, to unreality. The symbol is disincarnated. Concrete reality alone can bear no message. So a chimera must be created. Only the unreal can be an allegory.

The Hebrew on the contrary has recourse to daily facts, common reality, and history to signify and to teach the mysteries which are the proper food of our spirit.

In teaching us the *epourania*, the things of heaven, in describing the kingdom of God, Jesus, speaker of parables, uses as words the flesh of the most familiar realities: "A sower went out to sow his seed... A woman took leaven and put it into her flour... Unless the grain of wheat die... Of the fig tree learn this parable..." He never has recourse to myth, to allegory or to legend, for existing reality already has sufficient content to signify the mysteries which must be revealed. There is nothing more contrary to the Hebrew mentality and to its entire conception of the sensible and of contemplation than the Platonic type of allegorism which, too frequently, the Fathers of the Church confused with biblical typology. * The allegory rests on a dichotomy between being and meaning, and on a conventional relation between the sign and its content, whereas biblical typology rests on the belief that, historical fact itself is pregnant with meaning; so too is all reality, which is "word." *

A remarkable advantage of the Hebrew method of metaphysical and theological teaching, through parables built on sensible facts, is that it is universal. The *mashal* uses the most common and the most universally human things. It is not bound into some particular culture with its contingencies and its system of abstraction often reserved to an intellectual cast. To understand the language of the Bible one need only be human. The parables were plain to the Galilean peasant, and to the Corinthian stevedore in the days of St. Paul, as they are to the Western European worker or to the Chinese peasant of today. Perhaps we should add: especially to those. For unfortunately, a greco-latin humanist culture may very often prevent one from understanding the parables. They suppose an empirical familiarity with reality and with work, and they also suppose a love of the sensible which a Platonist mentality cannot have, because it is more or less

---

* Because they did not understand this fact some people have attempted to deny the historicity of the Gospel of John by pointing out that the events described are too full of theological meaning. The dilemma: either the Fourth Gospel is a historical narrative, in which case it could not contain a theology, or the stories contain a theological teaching, in which case they cannot be a recording of history. The dilemma is based on a premise to which many of us might spontaneously subscribe: "history belongs to the factual order and therefore is excluded from the intelligible order." This premise is an expression of dualism which is at the root of Greek philosophy. In Chapter VI we shall examine more attentively how history can be meaningful.

The Gospel of John (following in this the entire Semitic biblical tradition), explores and clarifies the significance of each act and movement of the Logos made flesh. And how could any act (no matter how humble) of the incarnated Logos not be charged with meaning? John is more the theologian than the other evangelists because he attentively follows the Son of Man to unfold all the *"semeia,"* all His acts which are signs.

unconsciously dualistic and too unfamiliar with the elemental to understand its depth and riches.

Because they hardly reflect any contingent cultural patterns, the parables can be universally understood, proceeding, as they do, to the revelation of the intelligible universal contained in the individual and the material. Biblical symbolism is universal because it is uncompromisingly concrete. It speaks the language of common people.

* * *

From each of these metaphysical doctrines two different conceptions of contemplation and of love will naturally follow.

To the Platonist contemplation and love is an elevation from the sensible to the archetype which the sensible represents. In biblical tradition contemplation is also an ascension from the sensible which is a word. But this is where the ways part. According to Plato and Plotinus one should flee the world. Biblical contemplation, on the contrary, admits the concrete and the particular. It proceeds by their mediation.

Platonic eros lifts itself from some particular and sensible beauty to another beauty less particular, until it reaches the universal and intangible Beauty from which all sensible and particular beauties proceed. This or that body's beauty is a participation, a partial reflection of Beauty itself. The Platonic lover loves, not such or such a particular being, but that Beauty which he glimpses through it and which brings him to contemplation through reminiscence of the universal. The loveliness or beauty of any individual is only an allusion which calls to the lover's mind that Beauty "yonder." Hence fidelity to true Beauty will be unfaithfulness to any particular beloved. The latter can only be a step, a stage. We must take leave, we must flee, to reach the object of our desire.

Don Juan, whom no woman can satisfy, is in that sense a Neo-Platonist. A woman's face leads him to contemplation. His love is the Platonic eros. What he loves is no one woman but some archetypal Feminity of which each woman bears in herself an ever incomplete reflection. Don Juan pursues the essence. What he calls love, means to abandon each woman whom he meets, in order to set off in pursuit of that one Beauty to which he is faithful.

Christian love, on the contrary, is a love for particular beings. The opposite approaches of Christian and Platonist to the sensible world and to the particular lead them to these very different conclusions on the nature of contemplation and of love.

* * *

The poetics of the Bible rests on its metaphysics of the sensible, and flowers out of it.

Sensible reality was created, and created by the Word. The sensible is essentially significant. Dualism is necessarily anti-poetic because it sentences the sensible to being meaningless. A dualistic anthropology will deny that human love and sensible union are a manner of knowledge. Whereas in the Bible, this we shall see, the union of man and woman is an initiation into the greatest of mysteries because the body is nothing other than the living soul. Dualism disrupts analogy and it is analogy which is the principle of biblical poetics.

The very fact that Hebrew metaphysics reveals itself under the appearances of the concrete sensible explains why it is poetic and reveals the nature of this poetry. It is poetic because there is no separation of sensible reality from the intelligible: the former is a revelation of the latter. So metaphysics and poetry are not divided. Poetry is knowledge and all knowledge is poetic.

* * *

Israel has no esthetics.

"If you raise an altar to me you will not build it out of carved stones, for if you lift your chisel to the stone you will profane it." [1] "Out of unhewn stones you will build the altar of Yhwh." [2] It was Israel's purpose to free the world of idols: "you will make no hewn image, no figure of which is above in heaven, or below on earth, or in the waters beneath the earth." [3] Israel is pure (kadosh) of anthropomorphic tendencies. "Because you did not see a shape on the day that Yhwh spoke to you from the midst of the fire on Horeb, take care of your soul lest you pervert yourselves and make some carved likeness, figure of some idol, likeness of man

---

[1] Ex: 20: 25.   [2] Deut. 27: 6.
[3] Ex: 20: 4.

or woman, likeness of any animal which lives upon earth, likeness of a bird which flies in the heaven, likeness of a beast which crawls on the ground, likeness of a fish which lives in the waters beneath the earth." [1]

Israel went off in search of that invisible and subsisting Beauty from which all beauty in heaven and on earth proceeds. Israel left no monuments for the museums: after all the splendid halls devoted to Egypt, Assyria and Persia, we find Palestine represented only by a hoe and a batch of tools, symbols of the poverty in which Israel goes towards the Beauty whose Name is wonderful. No monuments and no remains because all is transported, all assumed. This scarcity of artefacts is a consequence of the great tension of contemplative life. For Israel knows that land of beauty flowing with the spiritual milk and honey of the Word is not to be found here. [2] "For we are before you as strangers and travelers as all our fathers were." [3]

Because Israel has understood that beauty is Someone, she does not make monuments of beauty with her hands.

The artist makes an image of subsisting beauty. Through this image he himself finds access to beauty and shows the way to others. The image which he creates proceeds from a beauty of which he has inner knowledge, an intuition. The work of art stands as an aid to his contemplation.

The contemplative who needs no image to go to beauty produces no work of art. He goes to beauty without assistance from the work of the artist which is made to lead towards contemplation. His attention is strong enough. It needs no support. If he does not make a work of art it is not owing to indifference or inattention, nor because he is a stranger to beauty. It is because, through his contemplation, he is in personal relation with subsistent beauty, that the work of art is of no use to him. "The artist's point of view is therefore important, but not final." [4]

The poetry of the Bible is the flowering of its metaphysics. There is no biblical esthetics separate from, or added to, the metaphysics. None of the biblical authors sought literary beauty for its own sake; yet no man has ever written as these men wrote. The beauty of poetry was a gratuitous consequence of their contemplation. There is no search for dramatic effects; yet we must recognize

---

[1] Deut. 4: 15.
[2] 1 Peter 2: 2.   [3] 1 Chron. 29: 15.
[4] Bergson, *L'Energie spirituelle*, p. 25, P.U.F. 1946.

the tragic power in this stark language whose words rise out of silence and come to us through desert lands from men who know that all is vanity.

It is noteworthy that these texts remain poetic even in a translation. True poetry is a form of knowledge. Poetry lies in the meaning. The form proceeds from, is a result of, the fulness of contemplation.

* * *

It is particulars which exist. The Hebrew thinks in terms of the existing particular; for the particular to him is not at all insignificant; it is a vehicle of meaning. To manifest truth God chose among all nations a particular people. His choice went first to a particular man, whose name was Abraham, at a particular time, in a particular place. The Incarnation in turn is a choice of the particular, of the real, with all its historical and geographical contingencies: a particular woman, a particular period, and a particular country with its social contingencies. God Himself becomes a particular person to us, a person with a name, a face, a story.

This choice of the particular to manifest universal truth, to teach what is by rights universal, is without a doubt the greatest, the outstanding scandal to a Greek intelligence.

From the Greek point of view there are too many particulars in the Books of Israel for their contents to be a metaphysics: too many proper names, too much geography, too many dates, and too much history. Too many contingencies: truth is necessary. Too many sensible things: truth is abstract. Too many real people: truth holds no personal preference. Too much geography: truth is beyond space. Too many historical events: truth is beyond time. Too many particulars: truth is universal. Why, they ask, should such a people rather than another, such a man, such a time, such a day and not another, be favored by a choice?

All our most deeply ingrained intellectual habits inherited from Greek philosophy are opposed to this idea that truth is to be reached through the existing particular, opposed to this *nativity* of truth, to this manifestation of truth in some particular concrete reality. This method, which is the "method" of the Incarnation, offends the deep, congenital dualism of our minds, a dualism which establishes an essential distinction between the intelligible which belongs to the order of essence, and the existent, the order of fact, which is contingent and absurd.

We are told that there is too much history and geography, too many *facts* in the Scriptures for them to hold a metaphysics. The heart of the matter is that Scriptures *are a metaphysics and a theology in the form of a historical narrative.*

The Hellenic mind can never come to terms with the Incarnation, because of the antinomy which it places between the sensible, which is temporal, and the intelligible, which is timeless. Its Manichean conception of the sensible, its pessimistic conception of becoming, its view of time as a degradation of the timeless, its theory of individuation by matter and its ontology of the many and the one, and of the particular existent, all incline it to reject as unthinkable the coming into this world of Truth through a concrete, particular reality. Dualism is the contradiction of the method of the Incarnation.

chapter six

ISRAEL

Salvation comes from the Jews. [1]

The scandal of the Incarnation begins here. The assertion that the approach to truth and salvation must be through a particular people, definitely located in time and space, is the first premise of the scandal. No Greek philosophy can reconcile itself to this proposition.

True, in the Greek schools, the master taught his disciples, and in this sense truth used the mediation of a particular and contingent individual. But still the master was only a monitor, only recalled to mind a truth which the disciples already had within him. The master was a midwife, at most the teacher of a method. He transmitted a tradition.

"The method" of the Incarnation is different; it places truth itself within an existing particular — *"whom our hands have touched, our eyes seen"* — who is *"all the treasures of knowledge and wisdom."* So a man, a nation, becomes the *"door"* to the unseen truth that cannot be reached by any other way.

* * *

The concept of Israel is complex and ambiguous because it designates a reality which is also a sign.

Israel is defined by an alliance *(Berit)*. Whoever disobeys the commands of the Torah "will be cut off from the people of Israel." Conversely whoever is circumcised and obeys the Torah becomes an Israelite: "If a foreigner living among you wishes

---

[1] John 4: 22.

to observe the Pasch of Yhwh each man in his household will have to be circumcised. After that he will approach for the observance, and he will be as a native of the land." [1]   To be an Israelite is not really a matter of birth like being a Greek or an Egyptian. It is truly a matter of choice. Israel the nation does not cover the essence it implies. The Law and the Prophets defined it genetically, its true definition is spiritual.

What is the relationship, the dialectic between the empirical visible reality — Israel the ethnological fact — and its non-empirical, theological meaning — *verus Israel?* Those born into Israel only belong to it through individual choice. The two aspects of Israel do not coincide, or coincide only in so far as the nation is faithful to its theological calling. There is room for infidelity: it is the bark that is apparently a part of the tree though in fact it is separate, the sap does not flow through it. Every sign permits the possibility of falsehood.

Israel the nation is the symbol of a spiritual fact, and is in part also, part of that fact itself. Between its reality and its vocation we discover the theological dialectics of Israel and the passage from the Jewish nation to the Church. "...Not those who are Jews outwardly, nor those who are outwardly circumcised in the flesh, but those who are Jews in the spirit, whose hearts are circumcised in the spirit and not in the letter." [2]

It is this discrepancy between the visible and the invisible which can explain the ambiguous aspect of Israel. "Not all those descended from Israel are Israel. It is not because they are the posterity of Abraham that they are all his children." [3]   We find two aspects opposed in many places. On the one hand "Israel according to the flesh," *(Israël kata sarka),* [4] "those who call themselves Jews and are not so, but they lie," [5] and on the other hand the "Israel of God," [6] those who, like Nathanael, could be called "true" Israelites. [7]

* * *

---

[1] Ex. 12: 48.
[2] Rom. 2: 28.
[4] 1 Cor. 10: 18.
[6] Gal. 6: 16.

[3] Rom. 9: 7.
[5] Apoc. 3: 9; 2: 9.
[7] John 1: 48.

Very often, too often in fact, people will oppose the Old Testament to the New: one the exacting law, the other the rule of love. And so they echo an old heresy, Marcion's.

Truth lies the other way, in fact. From the Old Testament to the New we move, not to leniency, but rather to greater rigor. Let us see why.

The confusion which opposes the Old Testament to the New is founded on another confusion concerning the nature of love. Rigor and love are but one and the New Testament carries rigor of love to its most exacting application. Love is no compromise.

The New Law effects what mathematicians call a *generalization*. Having studied a function or statistical curve in relation to some particular case the mathematician *extends* its application to all possible cases.

The Old Testament Law dealt with empirical acts: murder, theft, adultery, etc. The New Testament now applies the law to all of human conduct; not only to visible acts but also to what is secret and invisible. So the old commandments are carried to interior regions hitherto unvisited — to the heart, and its secrets, and its freedom. The Old Law has not become tender, rather its rigorous measures have reached out to rule the furthermost and innermost human actions.

"Do not think that I have come to abolish the Law or the Prophets; I have not come to abolish but to complete them *(plērōsai)*... For not a single dot or comma of the Law will pass." "....You have heard that it was said to the people in the old days, 'Thou shalt not murder, and anyone who does so must stand his trial. But I say to you that anyone who is angry with his brother... You have heard that it was said, 'Thou shalt not commit adultery.' But I say to you that every man who looks at a woman lustfully....'' [1]

The demands of justice are made thoroughgoing. "If your justice is not better than the justice of the Scribes and the Pharisees you shall not enter the Kingdom of Heaven."

Opposing the Old Testament to the New amounts to parting justice and love. Here language holds a lesson for us: *zedaqah* in Hebrew means *both* justice and love.

How has the Law been changed?

Circumcision, for instance, is not abolished: the application of the Law goes further than ever before. Though the ritual sign

[1] Matth. 5.

is forgotten the content remains. The old sign held a meaning: "Be circumcised for Yhwh, take off the foreskin of your heart." "Yhwh will circumcise your heart." [1] While extending the meaning of circumcision to enclose terribly rigorous requirements the New Testament discards the visible sign, for "true circumcision is not that which is visible in the flesh. True circumcision is that of the heart: spiritual rather than literal." [2]

And so the question is raised: what is the essence of the sign, and what is the essence of language? Here the Church and the Pharisees would not agree. Christian exegesis of the Old Testament considers pharisaism an obsession with the letter, an inversion of meaning. Letter, language, sign require us to leave them as we move onward, through them, to the fact they imply; such is the drift of intelligence. Of the Pharisees Paul writes: "I will testify that they are devoted to God, but not according to (true) understanding." *(Ou kata epignōsin).* [3]

Under the Old Law the transgressor was "cut off from the people of Israel," exiled or stoned. The New Testament carries the sanction to the spiritual level, applies what the Old Law implied. Physical exile is no longer the sanction, nor is bodily execution. Today's offender is "cut off from Israel for eternity." The penalty is infinitely harsher, the image has given way before the ineluctable demands of life and love. "It is terrible to fall into the hands of the living God." *

**

           * * *

Israel is the mutant of a new species.

All new biological creation must grow from a germ. And so the birth of this new species, this spiritual nation — "nation of priests" — like any birth started from an infinitely small germ, a tribe, less than a tribe, a single man: Abraham.

---

[1] Deut. 30: 6.   [2] Rom. 2: 29.
[3] Rom. 10: 2.

* The logical link between justice (wrath) and love is jealousy. "I, your God, the Lord Almighty am jealous in my love" (Ex. 20: 5). "Yhwh your God is a fire that burns all before it, loves you with a jealous love" (Deut. 4: 24). "The whole earth shall be consumed with the fire of my jealous love" (Soph. 3: 8). "Not death itself is so strong as love, nor the grave itself cruel as love unrequited" (Song of Songs 8: 6). "The jealous fire" (Hebr. 10: 27). "Most jealously he loves the spirit which he has put within you" (James 4: 5). It is this relentless love that commands us to be saints.

The Church, too, grew from a handful of men. "What is the Kingdom of God like? To what shall I compare it? It is like a grain of mustard seed which a man took and dropped in his garden. It grows and becomes a tree and the birds come and nest in its branches." [1] The Kingdom of God did not add itself to the world from without. It was born within the world, sown in the world, and grows from it. "It is like the yeast which a woman took and covered up in three measures of flour until the whole lot had risen.' [2] "The Kingdom of God is like a man throwing seed on the ground; thereafter whether he sleeps or whether he wakes the seed sprouts and grows up, but he does not know how it happens.' [3] Israel *is a seed*, "If the Lord has held you closely to Him and chosen you, it was not that you surpass other peoples in greatness, of all nations you are the smallest." [4]

About 4,000 years ago Abraham left Ur in Chaldaea. "Yhwh said to Abraham: leave your country, your kindred and your father's home and come away into a land that I will show you.... Abraham went." [5] Every growth starts with a separation. And so the genesis of this new nation — this "mutation" — is accomplished by a departure. The spiritual adventure begins with exile. The first deed of Israel, a deed thereafter constantly repeated, is a leave-taking. "You that are my own people separate yourselves from her neighborhood; flee from the confines of Babylon, flee for your lives; would you meekly accept her punishment?" [6] "Flee, Israel, from Babylon, from Chaldaea's land be foremost to depart." [7] "Away from Babylon." [8] "Return, return, no more of Babylon." [9] "Go out from the midst of her, my people, take no part in her sins." [10]

To Israel, exodus is a permanent fact.

"I, Yhwh, your God, have set you apart among all the nations of the world... to belong to Me." [11] "It is not for you to live by the customs of that Egyptian land in which you once dwelt, or to imitate the men of Chanaan, the new home I am giving you, and follow their observances. It is My decrees you will execute, My commandments you will obey, following them closely; am I not Yhwh your God?" [12] "It is not for you to imitate the practice of

[1] Luke 13: 18.
[2] Luke 13: 21.
[3] Mark 4: 27.
[4] Deut. 7: 7.
[5] Gen. 12: 8.
[6] Jer. 51: 45; 51: 6.
[7] Jer. 50: 8.
[8] Is. 48: 20.
[9] Is. 52: 11.
[10] Apoc. 18: 4.
[11] Lev. 20: 24.
[12] Lev. 18: 3, 4.

the nations I am driving out to make room for you. Was it not these very practices that made Me their enemy?" [1]

From the very start God commands His people not to conform, to disobey the laws of the world. Israel is set apart, much as, now, the Church is set apart. "Here is a people destined to dwell apart, not counted among the muster-roll of the nations," Balaam pronounces, "Jacob needs no soothsayer, Israel no divination. In time Israel and Jacob will hear what God wills to accomplish." [2]   The separation of Israel from other nations is a condition of her prophetic mission; it is a result of her having been chosen by God. "You will be My people from out of all the nations for all the world is mine; but you will be for me a kingdom of priests and a holy nation." [3]

The constant temptation of Israel was to refuse this separation, this special vocation, and to return to Egypt for fear of the desert. "None of that will happen, that you say to yourselves; we shall be as other nations, like other folk on earth, servants to wood and stone." [4] "I shall make you go out from the midst of nations; I shall assemble you from the lands in which you have been dispersed by a strong hand, by an outstretched arm and an outspread wrath, and I shall lead you into the desert of nations and enter into judgment with you face to face." [5]

The desert years are the years of Israel's purification. The desert is a place for revelation. There Israel is stripped of the customs of nations and, with manna for food, remains completely dependent upon God. Before she may enter the holy land she is prepared to meet God by this mystical purification, during which God observes, weighs, and comes to know her: "I have known you in the desert, out in the dry land." [6] The silent desert allows for that first condition of understanding: attentiveness: "Therefore I shall draw her out and lead her into the desert and speak to her heart... and she will answer me as in the days of her youth, as in the day when she went out of the land of Egypt." [7]

We find this "theology of the desert" elaborated in the writings of St. John of the Cross.

* ** *

---

[1] Lev. 20: 23.   [2] Lev. 32: 23.
[3] Ex. 19: 5, 6.   [4] Ezech. 20: 32.
[5] Ezech. 20: 34, 35.   [6] Hos. 13: 5.
[7] Hos. 2: 16, 17.

Exile and wandering appear as Israel's permanent state. These facts are meaningful because they are a part of the nation's spiritual reality; its peculiar "metaphysical" make-up makes its history something eternally significant and *prophetic*. For Israel is not just a nation of men but also a theological fact born with Abraham and still thriving within all those who live as part of this new *spiritual* breed.

So there is exile and, beyond it, the lot of the stranger. "We are before you foreigners and wanderers like our fathers; our days on earth pass like a shadow, there is no hope." [1] "You will build no house but you will live in tents all your days, that your days may be long on this earth where you are strangers." [2] "You will not sell the land in perpetuity; the land is mine and you are in it as foreigners and passers-by." [3] Jacob speaks of "my years of pilgrimage" [4] and God for long years had no temple, but a tent: "In no house have I lived since I rescued the sons of Israel from Egypt; in a tabernacle, I traveled beneath a tent." [5]

These thoughts, frequently found in the Old Testament, appear in the New Testament too. "We do not have our citizenship *(politeuma)* here but in heaven," Paul tells us. [6] And John says of the Word made flesh that he "set up his tent in our midst." [7]

The deed of the Exodus has a meaning; it is not only a historical fact but also a metaphysical reality.

The entire history of Israel is composed, as is Israel itself, of an empirical aspect and a metaphysical one, of a contingent actuality, recorded and past, and of a substantial sign which, far from being obsolete, appears to us more and more significant and *true* as history unfolds.

In this way the full content of the Old Testament remains meaningful and effective today, each event having kept its deeper, spiritual, relevance. What should we care about the storied towers of Babylon, the imperial dreams of Pharaoh, the wars with the Philistines, the captivity in Babylon? But what has passed away is only the sensible sign; the inner meaning of the sign remains.

When the mathematician, for instance, has examined a function in some particular case, he can go on to a generalized function. At this stage he forgets the individual case which he no longer

---

[1] I Chron. 29: 15.
[2] Jer. 35: 7.   [3] Lev. 25: 23.
[4] Gen. 47: 9.   [5] 2 Sam. 7: 15.
[6] Phil. 3: 20; cf. Hebr. 11: 9 ff.; I Petr. 11: 11.
[7] John 1: 14.

needs, since, in the generalization he holds its "essence." Thus the wars and wanderings and captivities shed their garment of contingency in order to show us the spiritual truth we must learn.

The Exodus goes on, no longer in an empirical, but in an interior and spiritual, and therefore more real sense. War with the Philistines is no longer the battle against a nation which once opposed Israel; it is now the endless fight with the Philistines scattered among all nations, who are the enemies of the spiritual Israel. This spiritual war is much more merciless and awesome. Our concern is not with the Babylon of Nabuchodonosor, but with the Babylon whose name is a "mystery." [1]   Egypt and Assyria stood for another enemy. Now the sign has been transformed into reality. And on its fulfilment the empirical sign has passed away: "Yhwh shall reveal Himself to Egypt; and Egypt will know Yhwh.... In that day Israel will ally herself as a third party to Egypt and Assyria.... Yhwh will bless them saying: 'Blessed is Egypt, my people, and Assyria the work of my hand, and Israel my heirloom.' " [2]

The historical wars belong to the past: they are over and done. But the spiritual war, of which the historical wars were a sign, goes on, sometimes with real persecutions, between Israel and "the great city whose name in a spiritual sense is Sodom and Egypt." [3]

Under the New Law, the war, like the exodus and all the events of the Old Testament, is carried inwardly, spiritually, to its fullest significance. The Old Testament wars were real wars; but they were figures of another war, more merciless yet: "Do not think that I have come to bring peace on earth; I came not to bring peace, but a sword." [4]

Characteristically, all the realities which grow and ripen in time gradually shed that part of themselves which is temporary, in order to show themselves for what they are. Thus the New Law discarded like a chrysalis the signs which time has rendered obsolete. Now the message could be told plainly, instead of being told in parables.

* * *

"Now these events have become prototypes *(tupoi)* applicable to ourselves..." says St. Paul. "All these things which happened

---

[1] Apoc. 17: 5.   [2] Is. 19: 21 ff.
[3] Apoc. 11: 8.   [4] Matth. 10: 34; cf. Luke 12: 51.

to our ancestors were typical *(tupikōs)* events and they have been written down to be a warning to us upon whom the fulness of time has come." [1] We must learn to seek the *meaning* in the historical event, just as we read the *meaning* of a gesture.

Biblical history does contain, in the form of a historical narrative, an exposition of mysteries, of the theological truths which are a spiritual food. *Through history we absorb divine teaching.* Through history we come to contemplation. In fact, Christian contemplatives fed upon the biblical narratives to increase their understanding of mysteries. History is a *"musterion,"* a *"sacramentum."*

St. Bonaventure writes: "Sicut in Christum pie intendentibus aspectus carnis, qui patebat, via erat ad agnitionem Divinitatis, quae latebat; sic ad intelligendam divinae sapientiae veritatem aenigmatisis ac mysticis figuris intelligentiae rationalis manuducitur oculus. Aliter enim nobis innotescere non potuit invisibilis Dei sapientia nisi se his quae novimus visibilium rerum formis ad similitudinem conformaret et per eas nobis sua invisibilia, quae non novimus significando exprimeret." *

We find the same idea in St. Thomas: "Dicendum quod auctor Sacrae Scripturae est Deus, in cujus potestate est ut non solum voces ad significandum accomodet, quod etiam homo facere potest, sed etiam res ipsas. Et ideo... ipsae res significatae per voces, etiam significant aliquid." **

* * *

The same creative force which brought forth the worlds and the animal species is, today, the ferment of human events. The invention

---

[1] I Cor. 10: 6, 11.

* "Just as we, who look to Christ, come to the knowledge of his latent divinity through reverent contemplation of his patent humanity, so are we led through contemplation of the spiritual mysteries and symbols, to an understanding of divine wisdom, by the powers of rational intelligence. For the wisdom of the invisible God could not reveal itself to us otherwise than by taking up the shape of the visible objects with which we are familiar. In this way, by these signs, he reveals to us the invisible truth which we cannot perceive." (*De Plantatione Paradisi*, I, t. V, p. 575).

** "God, author of the Holy Scriptures, has power to give meaning, not only to words (man can do this), but also to all *things.* Thus in the Bible the very objects which words signify have a particular meaning" (*Summa Theol.* I, 1, 10. Cf. *Qdbt.* 7, a. 14). H. DE LUBAC, in *Catholicisme*, p. 133, puts it succinctly in Greek: Historika pneumatikôs, pneumatika historikôs" (The historical spiritually, the spiritual historically).

of new forms of life has ceased (*schabat*, says Genesis). God's creative activity is concentrated now at the summit of creation which is the human race.

Human history is a story of growth, development, an inward ripening. Mankind, throughout history to this day, is laboring as in childbirth. Something must come, will come from this fermentation, this pregnancy. *What* will come and *what* is being brought about is for the prophet to tell; for the prophet is a person who has an understanding of the direction of events.

Organic growth, the growth of plants and animals, is patient, gradual, continuous and calm. Not so the growth of mankind There are pangs of childbirth, brutal conflicts, contradictions, heartbreaking wars. To give a complete picture of the biblical philosophy of history we must not be content to stress the dynamic aspects of birth, and growth; we must also dwell upon the strongly negative and tragic element which is inherent in human development.

The philosophy of history held by the prophets of Israel is dialectical. The present period *('olam haze)* is one of war, the dialectic of oppressor and oppressed, of captivity in exile and return from exile; but, in time to come *('olam habah)*, the poor and the oppressed shall be set free. Peace is the fruit of a victory, of an ultimate liberation by a Liberator to come. "I shall bring back the captives of Juda." "The wolf will graze with the lamb." "I shall dry up all the tears of their eyes." History is moving toward something, it is moving toward peace. Peace is the term of human evolution.

We can see, how closely related to the ideas of Israel's prophets are the prime intuitions of Marx: history thought of as an evolution moving to the liberation of the proletariat, history guided from within by its own inescapable process, a process that is beyond the influence of any individual's will.

In the Bible, war, within the strict dialectic pattern of historical events, has a deep theological meaning. War, for Israel, is always the result of a breach of faith. The theological meaning of war which we find in the Bible seems best illustrated by the later development of the Church. At times the Church may lose sight of some portion of the truth with which she is entrusted. Instantly an opponent is raised, a champion of the forgotten fragment, to attack the Church on that count. Thus a morbid spirituality and a distortion of evangelical ethics raised and armed Nietzsche and

Freud. The fornication of Christianity with the rich, with temporal power, and with oppressors of the poor produced Marx. Truth cannot bear that any part of her be lost. She brings back to Christianity what negligence has scattered, brings it back with the sword, the rod of Yhwh, the man who is a hammer in the hand of God. If all of truth cannot find room within one Body, one Doctrine, she will obtain representation by several. That the many lovers of the single truth fight among each other bears witness to the oneness of truth. If doctrines rubbed elbows indifferently one might think them to be separate. But they contradict and oppose one another. "The harm that men do one another," writes Plotinus, "is caused by their aspiration towards good. Not reaching it they go astray and turn against one another." [1] War "means" that truth will not bear to be absent or divided. And truth does us this favor: she punishes our infidelity. She will not let us lose for good the deposit of justice which we hold. (The *Tsedaka*). We may depend on her, she will not stand to see us confirmed in error!

In this sense, throughout history, even our adversaries play a positive part in the economy of our salvation.

* * *

In history, as told by the Jewish prophets the Enemy is always a well defined figure of the day: Pharaoh, the King of Babylon, etc. So, too, the liberator: Moses, Samson, David, etc.

Behind these men, however, behind these familiar figures of past or present history, there arise, in the prophet's eye, another Enemy and another Liberator, to whom the historic figures are but vague approximations. And so takes shape the doctrine of an essential Enemy of Israel and an ultimate Liberator. In the prophetic sense, Pharaoh, Nabuchodonosor, Nero or Hitler fill the same part. For each one, in history, has the same *metaphysical* and *theological* function of Enemies of the People of God. In effect, these many Caesars do have an "air de famille," and the historical situations are quite similar. The *same spirit* is active in them, the same intention drives them, one might say, When we witness a periodic reproduction of analogous situations sparked by similar actors, might we not suspect that beneath the recordable fact there lies an unchanging cause, a deeper strife, to which the wars

---

[1] PLOTINUS, *Enn.* 3: 2, 4.

of man are but blown spray? Caesar's hatred of Israel has repeated itself too many times throughout history for it not to be a sign of a profound spiritual antinomy which is truly a law of history.

This is the idea sketched by the Apocalyptic literature. Between the Prince of this World and the Liberator, a cosmic struggle is unfolding, which will become fully apparent only in the end of time.

One should recognize in human history a negative element which cannot be reduced to mere inertia of matter, nor to a pathological process that biology, psychology, or sociology could explain. There is, it seems, some unrelieved evil that weighs on history. Our own age is particularly well equipped with experience by which to understand or at least to perceive this irreducibly negative element that will not be explained away by any science, for it is of an order beyond the grasp of scientific appraisal. This unrelieved negative which cannot be turned to good, may we not, along with Christian tradition, name it the *diabolic*. If we are not to lose sight of many significant aspects of history we shall do well not to overlook this quantity, this *x*, endlessly active in doctrines, methods, and men, all disquietingly alike through changing circumstances.

Schism is significant in the same way. Heresy brings to light a trend that was latent from the start, an infection to be worked off. It is good that the hidden trend should come to light, for the Church becomes aware of it then and frees herself of it. *Oportet haereses esse*.

Heresy frees the Church. Just as history develops through wars, so theology develops by the struggle against heresies.

We have made use of the history of the Church in our effort to grasp the dialectic of the history of Israel because deep down the processes appear analogous. The prophets endlessly proclaimed that war, captivity and oppression were made necessary by the faithlessness of Israel, and that they fulfilled a positive and indispensable function in the economy of Israel's salvation.

Within history two powers are at work. The one negative and evil, the other positive despite the suffering it holds. Both are inextricably mingled and, Christ cautions us, they must be left to grow until the harvest is ripe.

In the history of human growth these two forces are always present. We must guard ourselves both against a Manichean condemnation of history, and against facile optimism which bypasses the truly tragic aspects of the birth of *humanity* within mankind.

chapter seven

THE INCARNATION

"...All the wealth of full understanding, the knowledge of God's mystery, Christ Himself, within whom are hidden all the treasures of wisdom and knowledge..." "for in Him full divinity is *bodily* enthroned." *(To plērōma tēs tēheotētos sōmatikōs).* [1]

This is the arduous peak to which the foregoing analyses have been leading us. The Hebrew conception of the sensible world, of time, history, individual existence, its rejection of dualism lead up to this keystone: the Incarnation; a keystone that secures the whole structure, that everything in the structure presupposes.

The Incarnation is the keystone of the Hebrew conception of the world. Everything in Hebrew thought is preadapted to it, informed by it from the start.

We have, throughout the foregoing efforts of analysis, attempted to clear away numerous conceptual hindrances in order to reach what is, we believe, the heart of biblical thought, that gives it originality and savor, the Jewish sense of the Incarnation and of the real presence. In this we have proceeded as a musician might do, unfolding variations that become gradually more transparent until at the end we hear the theme itself in its broadest, most fundamental statement. We too have gone about it in somewhat that order, and the Incarnation is the basic theme which allows us to understand the Hebrew vision of the world, of history, of tangible creation. In the light of the Incarnation the elements become intelligible, history becomes meaningful.

The Incarnation implies a certain conception of the sensible of concrete reality, of history. Dualism is at the antipodes of this conception. From the dualist point of view, the Incarnation will always seem an untenable paradox, an intellectual scandal.

---

[1] Col. 2: 2, 3, 9.

To the Greek mind the dogma of the Incarnation is the foremost scandal, one that comes up against its deepest, its most intimate prejudices, those by which it lives, those which determine its most primitive categories. It goes against those axioms which are most powerful because they are the least discussed; axioms which are the underlying postulates, the very roots of Greek philosophy. These axioms have never really been challenged or brought to light — which makes them all the more tyrannical. The Greek conceptions of time, of the one and the many, of becoming, and of history render impossible an understanding of the Incarnation.

A whole implicit problematics, a whole system of deep-rooted intellectual habits would have to be renewed, reversed, in order to allow a Platonist to understand the Incarnation. This is what St. Paul calls "a renewal of the intellect." [1]

We are given to understand that one definite person, known to history, "whom our eyes have seen, our hands touched," "bears within him all the treasures of wisdom and knowledge," that is to say, the whole intelligible world. Even more, we are told that this one man proclaims that *he* is *truth*, in other words, the universal. Such a claim is a scandal to the Greek intellect. To say that "bodily" within one man is found the "fulness of divinity" is to unite the extremes which Greek dualism divides, those antinomic realities which are the sensible and the intelligible.

It is this distinction between Greek and Hebrew, between Greek and Christian that St. Augustine most clearly draws in the seventh book of his Confessions, relating that he read "certain books of the Platonists translated from Greek to Latin. There I found argued, though not in so many words, but by many and various reasons, that in the beginning was the Word.... That, however, he came unto his own... I read not..., There I read further that the Word, God, was born not of flesh, nor of blood, nor of the will of man, neither of the will of flesh, but of God; but that the Word was made flesh and dwelt amongst us, I read not..."

* * *

To the Platonist or Neo-Platonist the Incarnation can only be a *downfall*. Starting with this assumption, three explanations are possible.

---

[1] Rom. 12: 2.

First, the Incarnation is a contradiction in terms, an absurdity. So Spinoza thought: "When it is said that God assumed human nature I have expressly given warning that I do not know what they are talking about. Indeed, to tell the truth it strikes me as being in no way less absurd than an affirmation to the effect that the circle has taken on the nature of the square." [1]

Second, the Incarnation is only an appearance; this is the early heresy of Docetism.

Third, the Incarnation is truly a downfall, but willed by God himself who tore Himself asunder, became to His own self a stranger — in Hegel's words: *Entzweiung, Entfremdung*, respectively — in order that He might find Himself again, through the mediation of the world and of history in a higher joy. To Hegel, the Incarnation, like creation, is "an alienation of the divine essence." Hence it must be overcome; to the rule of the son the "rule of the spirit" must succeed. These, are the very words of the first Christian Gnostics. For creation, Hegel believes, was a voluntary alienation of the absolute who went out of himself *(Entäusserung)*, to undertake the great odyssey of our world's history. The Incarnation prolongs the same movement which is called the "exile" by the Cabala. "He himself alienates himself, and by dying, reconciles to itself the absolute essence." [2]

The cross itself is willed by God, and the rending separation and solitude that cried out: *Eli, lama sabachtani*, "the calvary of the absolute spirit, without which he would be a lifeless solitude." [3] We may find this Gnostic theory of the Incarnation from earliest Christianity up to Boehme and the German philosophers who drew sustenance from the Cabala and from the Gnostic tradition.

Dualism, of whatever school, is brought to view the Incarnation as an alienation of God within "matter." Light comes down to shine where there is darkness and is lost, exiled in darkness. Such a creed creates new problems. Plotinus wonders what lured the souls, bewitched, into their bodies. The Incarnation is an even more paradoxical fall. Dualism, by opposing the tangible and the intelligible, opposes the body and the soul, and so distrust of "matter" leads at length to a condemnation of "the body."

In the next chapter we shall outline a biblical anthropology. Through this study we shall be able to free the Incarnation from

---

[1] Spinoza, *Epist.* LXXIII.
[2] Hegel, *Die Phänomenologie des Geistes*, II.
[3] *Ibid.*

this dualist interpretation by showing that it is not a "fall into matter" in the biblical perspective, and this simply because the Hebrew did not conceive of the duality of body and soul. What the Bible calls the "flesh" has no relation whatsoever to what we today, in common speech, or what Plato, Plotinus, and Descartes in the past, referred to as the "body." And so, by this study, we may correct any false interpretation that a latent dualist tradition may have caused us to attach to the New Testament proclamation: *"the Word was made flesh."*

Part two

AN OUTLINE OF
BIBLICAL
ANTHROPOLOGY

We have seen how Hebrew thought avoids the division of form and matter, thus giving to the sensible a power of meaning which makes it a universal language.

Similarly the biblical anthropology is characterized by:

(1) the absence of the body-soul dichotomy. This is of great consequence. We need only consider all that the application of Platonic dualism implies in metaphysics, epistemology, psychology, and even in biology, to foresee the great reversal that a non-dualist conception of man, (such as that, for instance, held by Aristotelian Thomism), would bring about.

(2) the appearance of an absolutely original dimension quite unknown in philosophy, a specific contribution of the Bible: *ruah*, what we call the Spirit. *Ruah* is translated as *pneuma* by the Septuagint, and it is this term which the New Testament, and particularly St. Paul, uses in a very precise sense. This new factor introduces a dialectic which, as we shall show, cannot be reduced to the Platonic antinomy of body and soul. This dialectic rules the relationship of man and the super-natural factor at work within him, that calls him to a life both naturally unforseeable and quite beyond his hopes. This and none other is the separation the prophets make when they distinguish man, a "living soul" (or "flesh" which means the same thing), and the "spirit." These St. Paul in turns names the "psychical," *(or* "carnal"), and the "spiritual."

chapter one

NO DICHOTOMY OF BODY AND SOUL

Confusion reigns about the idea of "body" as it does about the idea of "matter," and for the same reason. Within these notions several heterogeneous problematics clash.

(1) *dualism*, whether Platonic, Neo-Platonic or Cartesian: the body is a substance different from the soul.

(2) *Aristotelian and Thomist metaphysics:* the "body" is a point of view on the concrete reality of living man, his "matter" distinguished only in abstract analysis from his "form" (his soul). In other words "body" just like "matter" is not a *physical* concept but a *metaphysical* notion proceeding from an analysis of the *metaphysical* structure of reality.

(3) *modern psychology, biology and psychiatry:* thinkers in these areas tend more and more to reject the Cartesian dualism of soul and body, though they retain the terms of the Cartesian approach.

(4) *biblical anthropology* introduces a new dialectic, "flesh" and "spirit," quite unrelated to the Platonic dualism of body and soul. For the biblical concept of "flesh" corresponds, not to the Platonic *sōma* (body), but to *the combination of sōma and psyche ("body" and "soul")*. Any confusion of the biblical distinction with Platonic dualism cannot fail to accentuate the latent Manicheism of substantial dualism, by the very fact that through this confusion we would attribute to "body" all that John or Paul wrote about "flesh."

* * *

What is the "body" according to the Platonist tradition?

"The illustrious Plato has said many beautiful things about the soul. In several places he speaks of its entry into this world and we may hope to draw something clear from this. What does this

philosopher say? It will appear that he does not always say the
same thing, in such a way that one might clearly see his meaning.
True, he always shows contempt for the sensible and makes
of the union of the soul with the body a reproach. He says that
the soul is in fetters, that it is in the body as in a tomb, and that
the Mysteries speak a great truth in saying that the soul is in prison.
Plato's cave and the cavern of Empedocles represent I believe,
our world, wherein progress towards intelligence is the soul's
deliverance from its bonds and ascent out of the cave. In the
Phaidros it is the loss of its wings that causes the soul's coming
here below. It rises again, but the end of a period brings it back
down. Judgments, lots, fate or necessity drive other souls down
here. According to all these passages the soul's entry into the
body is something reprehensible." [1]

"The body is a tomb," [2] says Plato, *(to sōma estin ēmin sēma)*,
and again: "as long as we have our soul kneaded into this evil thing
(meta tou toioutou kakou) we shall never possess in sufficiency
the object of our desire." [3]

The soul must isolate itself within itself and throw the body
from it, "as far as possible breaking all contact with it, fleeing
from it." [4] "...if ever we are to know something purely *(katharōs)*,
we must stand aside from it and let the soul in itself look upon
things in themselves." [5]

"...as long as we live we will be closest to knowing when, as
far as possible, we have no association or trade with the body
except as necessity compels, when we are no longer contaminated
by its nature but purified of its contact... attaining purity at last
in separation from the body's madness..." [6] "But is not purification,
in fact, just what the ancient tradition (Orphism) says it is: to
put the soul apart from the body as much as possible, to accustom
it to draw away, to collect upon itself foresaking every part of the
body in order to live isolated and alone as much as it can, and
completely detached from the body as though freed from its
bonds?" [7]

"Is not the exact meaning of the word death that a soul is unbound
and set apart from a body?" [*] "Other men do not suspect

---

[1] PLOTINUS, *Enn.* 4: 8, 1.
[2] *Gorgias*, 493 a.
[3] *Phaedo* 66 b.
[4] *Phaedo* 65 d.
[5] *Phaedo* 66 d.
[6] *Phaedo* 67 a.
[7] *Phaedo* 67 c.
[*] *Phaedo* 67 d; 64 c; *Gorgias* 524 b: Death is merely the separation of two
distinct things, soul and body."

that the sole occupation of any man who lives philosophy in the right sense, is to die and to be dead." *

One must take care not to read the same dualist meaning into the Aristotelian and Thomist theory of matter and form. "Body" here is not a *substance* — no more than "matter" is — but merely a *point of view* on that concrete reality, living man. The body is man *looked at* from a certain angle.

Indeed, when the "soul" is gone, what remains is not a "body" but a corpse, the dust of disjoined elements which only provisionally, as though by reprieve, retain the deceptive appearance of a living body. A corpse is not even a thing in the philosophical sense: it is a *heap*. "The dead finger, for instance, is only a finger in name." [1] "The eye is the matter of sight. If sight fails we no longer have an eye except in name, as with a stone eye or a painted eye." [2]

What we call the "body" in post-Cartesian philosophy was called the concrete and sensible whole by Aristotle. This living and sensible whole is not, to Aristotle or St. Thomas, the body, but the man. No more than "matter" can "body" be pointed out. It is not a physical, but a metaphysical, reality.

It is characteristic of dualism that it conceives two things where there is only one, and sees the body as something *other* than man. Descartes always speaks of the body as of a stranger.

In a living organism there *is* a *potential* multiplicity within a real unity, but it is only potential and abstractly conceived. This potential multiplicity is the "matter," the "body" of the concrete living being. Death makes real this potential multiplicity *seen in* a living organism. While it might perhaps be conceded that the corpse is a thing, we can never say that the body is a thing. It is a metaphysical, not an empirical, *view* of a multiplicity which is potential, which will come, but which is not real as long as the man lives.

Descartes always speaks of the body as of a stranger. The body as he defines it is just what we have said, the potential corpse

---

* "The reason for (all these errors) is that people look for a unifying formula and a difference between potentiality and actuality. But, as we have said, the proximate matter and the shape are one and the same; the one existing potentially and the other actually. Therefore, to ask the cause of their unity is like asking the cause of unity in general; for each individual thing is one, and the potential and the actual are in a sense one." (ARISTOTLE, *Met.* H, 6, 1045 b, Loeb, Oxford).

[1] ARISTOTLE, *Met.* Z, 10, 1035 b, 25.
[2] *De Anima*, 2, 1, 412 b, 20.

seen in the living man: "First I considered myself, having a face, hands, arms, and this whole machine of bone and flesh such as we see it in a corpse. To these I gave the name of body." [1]

The postulates of substantial dualism lead to the assertion that living man is made of his corpse to which a unifying form has been added: the *sundesmos*, the soul as a bond. This is an inversion of reality. Again we find the confusion of fabrication and creation. In speaking of the world this confusion produced the concept of substantial matter from which were shaped the sensible realities. In the case of man it leads to the concept of a body, distinct from the soul, and to the idea of a substantial duality within man.

But in fact an organism always grows from unity. True, man in the concrete is composed of an agglomeration, a "dust," of bio-chemical elements and of a soul that unites them. But it unites them, not artificially, but by assimilating the sundry elements, making them other than they were. In the living man the unity comes first. Sensible man is a unity of living soul and elemental dust, but as long as he lives he *is* not dust. Life's end brings dust to dust. Breath gone, gone the love that bound them, gone the life that made all dust to serve it, the lifeless elements past usefulness, and no longer drawn together by any living purpose, fall back into dust.

If we still wish to use the word "body" in any concrete anthropology, then we must not say: man is composed of a body and a soul; but: the living body that is man is composed of the dust of organic elements, and of a soul that informs them.

* * *

Language itself often has metaphysical implications. In Hebrew there is no word for "body."

"To the Accadian and to the Hebrew the body is not a "rag" that one despises and from which one seeks riddance. They were even rather reluctant to separate it from the soul which quickens it. It is known that expressions, applying to the body in general as distinguished from the soul, were early on reserved to the corpse. Thus in Hebrew the word *gouph* which nowadays means "body," appears only in the feminine gender in the Bible: *gouphah* "corpse." *Gewyyāh* too, usually means "corpse" rather than the living body...

---

[1] DESCARTES, *Méditations*, II, AT. IX, p. 20.

The tendency to reserve the generic term of body to the dead is already found in Assyrian. Here the word *pagru* which originally meant "body," eventually came to designate the corpse. It is with this meaning that it was adopted in Hebrew: *pheger*.

"When the Hebrew spoke of the living body, the body shaped by God in the womb, they used the word *bāśār*, "flesh." It was distinguished from *śe'er* which had less broad a meaning and signified rather the meat, the fleshy parts of the body. The expression *Kōl bāśār* "all flesh" meant all human beings." [1]

Festugière points out that in the New Testament "there being no Hebrew word for body, *sarx* stands for the word *bāśār* which means flesh... * *Sōma* for Matthew, Mark and John, designates the dead body, the corpse." *

* * *

Man was created. The multitude of men does not proceed from fragmentation of God's primeval unity, from an alienation of God in a multiplicity that pre-existed within his oneness. It is the fruit of positive *creation*. Not an illusion which death dispels by again blending brief time's multiplicity into the eternal unity from which it came; not an alienation willed by the Absolute himself in order that he might find again, after his odyssey had come to an end, a more perfect oneness and a consciousness richer for having overcome the primal sundering; the multitude of men is the fruit of a positive act that leaves the Creator's transcendency unaffected. Again we mark this: neither immersion, nor exile, but creation.

There are some corollaries to this view.

I. The problem of evil is, in the Bible, explored from man's point of view, by the sufferer from the sufferer's point of view. And so it is thought out with "infinite passion," as Kierkegaard says, by the "private thinker" Job.

To any metaphysics in which the creation of beings is replaced by an alienation of the Absolute in multiplicity, and in which

---

[1] E. DHORME, *L'emploi métaphorique des noms de parties du corps en hébreu et en akkadien*, RB, 1920, pp, 470-1.
* Cf. Matth. 19: 5; 26: 41; Mark 10: 8; 14: 38; Jo. 1: 14; 6: 33, 51; 1 Pet. 4: 2; Matth. 5: 29; 14: 12; 19: 5; 32: 58; Mark 10: 8; 15: 43; Jo. 19: 31, 38, 40; 20: 12. A. J. FESTUGIÈRE, *L'idéal religieux des Grecs et l'Evangile*, 1932, p. 196, footnote.

creation is only an appearance, evil likewise can only be an appearance. To the Gnostic Docetism which discards creation, there corresponds a Docetism of suffering and of evil. Suffering is no longer seen in terms of the individual. The explanation starts from the universal instead. In Hegel's cosmology, the great invention of the Absolute is that he tore himself apart to undergo the tragic adventure of his exile among the multiplicity of beings. This adventure leads to the "calvary of the absolute spirit, without which he would be a lifeless solitude," and beyond which he finds himself again, all dissonance overcome — *felix culpa* — in the higher joy of the final concord that justifies the tragedies of history. So evil is *esthetically* justified. Already Plotinus [1] considered suffering and evil, *spectacles*. Suffering is made unreal, its content is denied in order that it may become intelligible. Leibnitz in turn makes evil a dissonance justified by the symphony's final consonant chord. This notion haunts the philosophies of Leibnitz, of Hegel, and all of German romanticism: tragedy is a musical element, indispensable to the beauty of the cosmic symphony. The real world is equated to a musical phenomenon. What is the monadology, if not a symphony composed of living and subsistent notes which, by the infinity of their points of view, multiply the original opulence of the divine Music, *Monas Monadum*, for its greater delectation?

The secrete theme of the Gnostic cosmogony is that dissonance, evil, is the indispensable motor of that symphony which is the world's history, a history as irreversible as music. Tragedy is the key to it. The birth of tragedy and the birth of this music are the evil in the world's beginning. Sin is the artifice chosen by the Absolute to enhance the glory of the pan-symphony that he is. Evil is justified by music. Let us recall the text of the Phenomenology which clearly expresses this esthetic requirement: "Das Leben Gottes und des göttlichen Erkennen mag also wohl als ein Spielen der Liebe mit sich selbst ausgesprochen werden; diese Idee sinkt zur Erbaulichkeit und selbst zur Fadheit herab, wenn der Ernst, der Schmerz, die Gedult und Arbeit des Negativen darin fehlt." *

As there is no place for the creation of individual and personal beings in Gnostic Pantheism, the sufferings of individual men are transmuted, by an alchemy of the imagination, into noble tragedy

---

[1] PLOTINUS, *Enn.* 3: 2, 15.
* LASSON, p. 20. We have already given this text in English. See page 14.

and music, delightful to the Absolute.   In this way, and at small expense, the rose is set within the cross.

II.   Love, in the Bible's metaphysics, goes to each existent, particular being.   Here stands the distinction of the biblical and Christian *agapē*, and the Platonic *eros*.   The term and concept of *agapē* are peculiar to biblical tradition: "Thou shalt love thy neighbor as thyself." [1]

For a metaphysics in which the individual results from a fragmentation of primeval oneness, love can only be a nostalgic desire of return to the lost unity.   The love of such or such a particular being for its own sake would be quite meaningless; more than meaningless, it would be sinful, as an attachment to an illusory existence, that can only delay "conversion" to the One. The love of God for particular beings would be contradictory for the same reason.   "There cannot truly be love of God for something else, since all that is is one thing only: i.e., God Himself." [2]   Which gives us Spinoza's somewhat inverted definition of love: "Amor nihil aliud est quam laetitia concomitante idea causae externae." [*]

Tied in with the Docetism of creation we find a Docetism of love.

On the contrary, the biblical tradition firmly rejects any evasion of love toward the abstract universal.   To think that one loves God if one's love does not first go to individual existent beings, is a delusion.   "If anyone says: 'I love God,' but hates his brother, that man is a liar.   For anyone who does not love his brother, whom he sees, could not possibly love God whom he does not see." [3]

An unbreakable link definitely ties love of God to love of man: "Thou shalt love the Lord thy God... The second commandment is *similar* to the first: thou shalt love thy neighbor." [4]

* ** *

Man is created a "living soul."   "Yhwh God formed man from the dust of the ground and He blew into his nostrils a breath of life; and man became a living soul." [5]   What does this mean?

---

[1] Lev. 19: 18; Matth. 5: 43; 22: 39; Mark 12: 31, 33; Luke 10: 27.

[2] SPINOZA, *loc. cit.*

[*] Love is nothing else but pleasure accompanied by the idea of an external cause. (Eth. III, Prop. XIII, Schol., Trans. in PHILOSOPHY OF BENEDICT DE SPINOZA by R.H.M. Elwes, Tudor Publishing Co., N. Y.)

[3] 1 John 4.   [4] Matth. 20: 37-39

[5] Gen. 2: 7.

Once again we must be careful to avoid interpreting the Hebrew notion of soul in terms of Platonic dualism. Because they recognized no body-soul dichotomy the Hebrews did not consider the soul the disincarnate thing that we imagine it to be. And it is just because we oppose it to "body" that we think of it in this way. In Hebrew the soul is the man. Indeed we should not say that man *has* a soul, but that he *is* a soul; nor consequently that he has a body, but that he is a body. By applying to the Hebrew *Nephesch*, which the Septuagint translates by *psuchē*, the characteristics of the Platonic psyche, (conceived in the terms of a dualism of orphic origin), we let the real meaning of *Nephesch* escape us and furthermore, we are left with innumerable pseudo-problems.

Unhampered by the body-soul dichotomy, the Hebrew calls this tangible, sensible, expressive, and living reality that is man, a soul. I perceive, not a "body" which contains a "soul," but, directly, a living soul. Within the sensible that I am shown I may decipher all the wealth of its intelligibility. This soul is visible to me because it is within the world, fed on the world's elements which in turn cause it to *be* flesh. The essence of this flesh which is man, is the soul. The soul gone, there is no "body" left: nothing is left. Nothing but the world's own dust.

Again language confirms this.

For the living man, Hebrew uses indiscriminately the term "soul," *nepeš*, or the term "flesh," *bāśār*. Both of these point to one reality: earth-bound, living man, So too the expressions "all flesh," *Kōl bāśār*, and "every soul," *Kōl hanepheš*, are equivalent. *Kōl bāśār* first designates all the living, [1] then more precisely, all men. [2] In the same way *Kōl hanephes* designates all living beings. [3] "Every living soul," *Kōl nepheš ḥayah*. [4]

In the New Testament we find the same expressions and the same coincidence of meaning: *pasa sarx*, (all flesh), [5] and *pasa psuchē*. [6] Finally the expressions "to judge according to the flesh," [7] "to walk according to the flesh," [8] "to live according to the flesh," [9] must not be interpreted in terms of Platonism, in which sense

---

[1] Gen. 6: 13, 17; 7: 15, 21; Ps. 136: 25.
[2] Gen. 6: 12; Is. 40: 6; Jer. 25: 31; 12: 12; Zach. 2: 17.
[3] Jos. 10: 28, 30, 32, 35, 37.
[4] Gen. 1: 21, 24; 2: 7, 19; 9: 10, 12, 15; Lev. 11: 10.
[5] Matth. 24: 22; Mark 13: 10; Luke 3: 6; 1 Cor. 1: 23; Rom. 3: 20; Gal. 11: 16.
[6] Acts 2: 43; 3: 23; Rom. 2: 9; 13: 1; Apoc. 16: 3.
[7] John 8: 15.   [8] Rom. 8: 4.
[9] Rom. 8: 13.

they would mean: to satisfy the desires of one's body. In the Bible
these terms have a quite different meaning. To demonstrate this
we need but quote St. Paul who, with exactly the same intent,
uses the expressions: "to walk according to man," [1] and "to walk
according to the flesh." To say: "are you not carnal?" he just
as willingly writes: "are you not men?" [2]   "Can't you see that
as long as there is jealousy and squabbling among you, you are
carnal and walking according to man... are you not men?" [3]   In
this same text, instead of: "*ouk anthropoi este*," a variant proposes
"*ouchi sarkikoi.*" [4]   Nowhere do we find the word flesh used to
convey what we mean by "body."

Flesh is our index of frailty. The flesh is the man inasmuch
as he is not a god. The biblical distinction stands between the
Maker and those He made, not between body and soul, as in Plato.

* * *

All souls are created by God. Their multiplicity is willed for
its own sake, produced by a positive act. It is not the result of
an encounter of Unity with a material principle which divides
it *(chōra)*. *   Freed from the notion of matter, creation of the
multiple appears as a truly positive act instead of being the inversion
which Neo-Platonism depicts.

This brings us to the problem of individuation.

As we have seen Plotinus believed that the universal soul is
fragmented as it descends into bodies. Thereafter each particular
soul is preoccupied with its own body and so forgets its former
universal and one reality. "They descend from the universal
into its parts. Each soul wants to stand apart; it tires of being
with another; it withdraws within itself. Having remained at this
distance, separate from the whole and without turning its eyes
to the intelligible, the soul becomes a fragment, isolated, weakened,
its action multiplied and intent upon fragments. As it rests on
but one object apart from the whole, it goes ever further from
everything, turning itself towards this single object jostled by all
others. It leaves the whole and governs with difficulty, its own

---

[1] I Cor. 3: 3.   [2] *Ibid.*
[3] I Cor. 3: 4.   [4] Cf. Is. 57: 16; Jer. 38: 16.
* *Chōra* means both *space* and *matter*. It is derived from *chōrizein* which means
to separate.

particular object. It is now in contact with it and protects it from all outer objects, present to it and penetrating within it to a great extent." [1]   Individuation introduces care. The entrance into a body is its result, a fragmentation, a restriction as well as a servitude: "...as though, knowing all about some science we never considered but a single theorem... Likewise this soul... so to speak, leaps out from the universal being, and into a particular being upon which it directs a particular activity." [2]   Hence to become a particular being is an alienation, a fall, a negative process. "If you are in the universal being *(en tō panti)* you will look for nothing else. If you renounce it you will incline to something else, you will fall and no longer see its presence, because you look elsewhere. But if you seek nought else but him, how will you experience his presence? In that you are near to him and that you have not stopped at some particular being. You do not even say of yourself any more: that is who I am. You abandon all limits to become the universal being *(gegonas pas)*. Yet you were that from the start. But you were some thing else too and this surplus diminished you, for it did not come from being (one does not add anything to being), but from not-being. By this not-being you become somebody, and you are the universal being only if you abandon this not-being." [3]

"...Becoming man one ceases to be all. *   And one must cease being man in order to raise oneself, as (Plato) says, and to govern the whole universe. Having become sovereign of the universe one creates the universe." [4]

Likewise to Bergson individuation comes from a movement of inversion which is materiality. **   "The current (of life) passes through human generations, subdividing itself into individuals: this subdivision was already vaguely traced out, but would never have marked itself without matter. And so, ceaselessly, souls are created which, in a certain sense however, already pre-existed." [5]   As with Plotinus, individuation is an *"ensomatosis,"* a descent into a body. Plotinus makes his Fourth Ennead a treatise on the "descent of the souls into the bodies." On this same question Bergson writes: "If 'souls' exist, capable of an independent life, where do they come from? When, how and why do they enter

---

[1] *Enn.* 4: 8, 4.   [2] *Enn.* 6: 4, 16.
[3] *Enn.* 6: 5, 12.
* *Apestè gar tou einai to pan nun anthrōpos genomenos.*
[4] *Enn.* 5: 8, 7.
** Cf. Appendix, The Neo-Platonism of Bergson.
[5] BERGSON, *L'Evolution créatrice*, p. 270, P.U.F. 1946.

this body which we see, before our eyes, arising quite naturally from a mixed cell taken from the bodies of its two parents?" [1]

Like Plotinus, Bergson believes that bodily life is care-ridden. *
Along with individuation by matter, we find the same substantial dualism of body and soul, and a certain conception of salvation which is a return, or conversion, a detachment from care, and therefore a liberation from the illusion of the many.

On this point — individuation by matter — biblical metaphysics and metaphysics of the Neo-Platonic type stand in utter disagreement. No conciliation is possible and, on this one crucial question, Christian philosophy, which grows essentially and organically from biblical metaphysics, will have to face the Neo-Platonism that survives throughout all Western thought.

In the first chapter of this book we saw that, according to Hebrew thought, particular beings were created for their own sake; their multiplicity was willed; it was not a fall but a conquest of fertility. The entire Hebrew conception of the world is opposed to the idea of individuation by matter, since it ignores the very ideas of matter and of "body" as a substance other than the soul. We cannot fail to notice how profoundly consistent are the Bible's anthropology and its metaphysics of the sensible, the multiple and the particular. This metaphysics of multiple and particular beings, created for their own sake by a positive act, is the foundation of Christian personalism. And it is Bergson's doctrine of individuation by matter which makes his philosophy radically incompatible with the demands of Christian philosophy.

Thomism is often ambiguous on this point. Already with Aristotle, are we sure whether individuation is effected by matter or by form?**   In the case of St. Thomas, as in the case of Aristotle,

---

[1] BERGSON, *L'Evolution créatrice*, p. 269, P.U.F. 1946.

* On the subject of care, see the appendix on Bergson and Appendix II: *Care*.

** "That is an incoherence in Aristotle's system which cannot be denied... its weak point is his theory of individuation, a theory which is not at all required by the logic of the rest of the doctrine. Of the two conceptions of individuality which we find in the writings of Aristotle only one is compatible with the main principles of the Aristotelian thought: God's individuality comes to him because he is self-sufficient; it is because he possesses a fully sufficient positive reality that he is a separate being. On the contrary, the individuality of other individuals is explained by negative characteristics: the privilege of separate existence, in itself a sign of excellence and of positive reality, comes from a defect. This Platonic way of thought is understandable in Plato because he does not think very highly of the individual. But one cannot understand why Aristotle should have adopted it... to ask of matter an explanation of the positive part of an individual is to consider individuality as an infirmity" (HAMELIN, *Le système d'Aristote*, 1931, p. 106).

we may wonder, according to the texts invoked, whether or not matter is a substance, and whether the body is a substance (which would bring us back to Platonic dualism) or only the matter of man. It seems that on this point St. Thomas wavered between two conflicting metaphysical systems, and that Neo-Platonism often prevailed over the intrinsic requirements of Christian philosophy. *

Each individual is created for his own sake. The Hebrew metaphysics of individuation is illustrated by the significance of the proper name in the Bible. "I have known you by your name." ¹ God speaks to Jeremiah as to the particular being that he is: "before I formed you in the belly I knew you; and before you came forth out of the womb I sanctified you," ² for particular beings are willed and created for their own sake. Each one's name, each one's essence is unique and irreplaceable. Each being is, in the words of Laberthonnière, *apax legomenon*. The metaphysical lesson we may draw from the significance of the proper name is clearly at the counterpole from individuation by matter. It is the seed of Christian personalism.

It also allows us better to understand the metaphysical role played by historical individuals, the metaphysical importance of history, of men and of events which to the Greek mind are meaningless precisely because, in Greek thought, individuals have no ontological status which would allow them to fulfil any real metaphysical function.

In the Bible historic individuals Abraham, Pharaoh, Nabuco-donosor fill a metaphysical, and even a theological function. Their history is pregnant with theological teaching. Their birth and death have an importance which the prophet publishes. There is food for contemplation in the simple fact of the existence of David or of John the Baptist. Biblical history is the foundation of contemplation for the Christian mystics, a fact that would be difficult to justify or to explain, if this history were but an agglomeration of absurd and contingent facts. But, since the particular existent is intelligible, facts and individuals are not

---

* Upon this point Laberthonnière writes: "I am opposed to Bergsonism as radically as I am opposed to Aristotelo-Thomism and for the very same reason: it is because, though they contradict one another, they both include a theory of individuation which ignores and finally denies any consistency, any ontological reality, any value to the individuals that we are." *(Esquisse d'une philosophie personnaliste)*.

¹ Ex. 33, 12, 17: et saepe.   ² Jer. 1: 5.

unpalatable to the mind. Instead they are its food. Without the mediation of the particular there is no mystic knowledge.

* * *

Corresponding to these two basically different systems we find two different conceptions of sin and of salvation.

To Plato evil comes from the body that enslaves the soul to the sensible. The body is a rivet that holds us to this foreign land in which we are alienated. We must flee from here as soon as possible.

The Bible, on the other hand, proclaims the excellence of the created and the sensible. The origin of evil is to be found elsewhere and the carnal, not being its prime cause, is freed from blame. The cause of it is spiritual. The typical sin is the lie.

The Platonist believes the separate spirit to be necessarily good. Any being undefiled by contact with the sensible would be good by its very nature. The idea of evil angels appears nonsensical in the context of a Platonic system.

As regards the sensible and the carnal, Hebrew thought is therefore optimistic. But its metaphysics of evil opens perspectives much more tragic than those shown us by Platonism. Asceticism is not salvation, for evil is not born out of our physical existence. All sin is a *spiritual act* and ascetic practice cannot suffice to deliver us from evil. To biblical theology the Catharist movement was a heresy. The battle we strive to win is much more difficult.

Any confusion between the fundamentally different approaches these two systems represent is of weighty consequence. For a theology drawn from Revelation, it involves both a Manichean conception of the sensible quite foreign to the biblical postulate, and a loss of understanding of the supernatural which is the dimension peculiar to Revelation.

To these two systems which we have described, two wisdoms, two different doctrines of salvation, correspond. We can tell which wisdom we are dealing with according to the attitude it takes toward the sensible and the bodily. This is the touchstone to distinguish natural mysticism, natural wisdom from Christian spirituality.

If the multitude of beings is the result of a fall and fragmentation of the Absolute, then salvation will be conversion, a return to the lost unity, a departure from this bodily existence where our cares estrange us from God.

On the contrary, in the biblical metaphysics, in which the multitude of living souls is the fruit of positive creation, salvation cannot consist in undoing what this excellent creative act has done. Rather, salvation will continue in the same sense as the immanent creative act. Only in such a conception of the multiple and of individuality can a metaphysics of love have any meaning. Where the principles of individuation by matter or by inversion are accepted, love is really meaningless because it is reduced to a return to unity. In the biblical, and in the Christian sense, love is not the reabsorption of the many in the one. Instead, it is in the proliferation of created beings that love finds its fullest expression.

The doctrine of salvation found in biblical metaphysics is essentially supernatural. We shall discover the Christian meaning of supernatural when we analyze the biblical notion of spirit.

* * *

Because it ignores the Platonic body-soul dichotomy, the Hebrew language often attributes "bodily" functions to the soul.

The soul lives: "let my soul live to praise You." [1] And the soul dies: "let my soul die with the Philistines!" [2] "You would ensnare the souls of my people and your own souls would live?... You have dishonored me... causing souls to die that must not die." [3] In the New Testament we find the same expression: "Every living soul will die." [4]

One should note that, whereas the soul dies, we never read that *ruah*, the *spirit* dies.

In our dualist system it is the custom to attribute passions and organic functions to the body, and all that is of a psychological order to the soul. In Hebrew, because there is no dualism, passions, organic functions, sensations, are just as easily related to the soul as they are to the organs and, conversely, thoughts and sentiments are ascribed to the organs and to parts of the body.

My soul hungers [5] and thirsts. [6] "If your soul lusts after meat..." [7] "I shall give water to the thirsting soul, and I shall satiate the languishing soul." [8] "As the hart pants after the water brooks, so my soul pants after You, O God. My soul thirsts for God,

---

[1] Ps. 119: 175.
[3] Ezech. 13: 19.
[5] Ps. 107: 9; Prov. 10: 3; 27: 7.
[7] Deut. 12: 20; cf. Mi. 7: 1.

[2] Jud. 16: 30.
[4] Apoc. 16: 3.
[6] Prov. 25: 25.
[8] Jer. 21: 15.

for the living God." [1] "My soul thirsts for you, my flesh languishes after you in a dry land." [2] "I will satiate the soul of the priests with fat." [3] "To fill the soul" means to feed it. [4]

"The hungry man dreams that he eats, but he awakens and his soul is empty." [5]

"Our soul is dried away." [6] "Our soul has conceived a loathing for this miserable food." [7] "My soul is weary of life." [8]

The soul hears: "Do you hear, my soul, the sound of the trumpet." [9] The soul despises, [10] hates, [11] desires love [12] or vengeance. [13] The soul is afflicted: "Until when will you afflict my soul." [14] It blesses: "Let my soul bless you before I die." [15] The soul knows, [16] remembers, [17] and loves: "His soul clave to Dina, the daughter of Jacob, and he loved the girl." [18] "You whom my soul loves." [19]

In the New Testament the word "soul" is used in exactly the same manner: "Do not worry about your souls in regard to what you will eat and drink." [20] "You will find rest for your souls." [21] "The fruits that you desired are departed from you." [22] "My soul is troubled." [23] "My soul is sorrowful unto death." [24] "I shall say to my soul: my soul, you have many goods set aside for many years, so take your ease, eat, drink and be merry." [25] "Tribulation and anguish upon the soul of every man that does evil." [26]

Bodily functions are attributed to the soul. Conversely Hebrews leave their psychological role to the organs and to the parts of the body. On this point it concurs with modern psychology.

"His bowels did yearn." [27] "The bowels of the evil man are cruel." [28] "My bowels will tremble for joy." [29] "My bowels were moved

---

[1] Ps. 42: 2.
[3] Jer. 31: 14.
[5] Is. 29: 8.
[7] Num. 21: 5.
[9] Jer. 4: 19.
[11] Ps. 17: 9.
[13] Ps. 27: 12.
[15] Gen. 27: 4.
[17] Lam. 3: 20.
[19] Song of Songs 1: 7; 3, 1: 4.
[21] Matth. 11: 29.
[23] John 12: 27.
[25] Luke 12: 19.
[27] Gen. 43: 30; Reg. 3: 26.
[29] Prov. 23: 16.

[2] Ps. 63: 2.
[4] Prov. 6: 30.
[6] Num. 11: 6.
[8] Job 10: 1.
[10] Ez. 36: 5.
[12] Jer. 2: 24.
[14] Job 19: 2; Ps. 119: 28; Job 30: 16.
[16] Ps. 139: 14.
[18] Gen. 34: 3.
[20] Matth. 6: 25.
[22] Apoc. 18: 14.
[24] Matth. 26: 38; Ps. 42: 6.
[26] Rom. 2: 9.
[28] Prov. 12: 10.

for my beloved." [1]   "My bowels were troubled for him, yes, I shall have mercy on him — word of Yhwh." [2]

"My reins rejoice." [3]   "Even during the night my reins instruct me." [4]   The reins are that part of us in which arise the secret desires that we admit only reluctantly, even to ourselves, the obscure region that psychoanalysis uncovers.   God "sounds the reins and the hearts." [5]   The reins, in biblical psychology appear to represent more or less what modern psychology calls *libido*.

Hebrew psychology of the passions and emotions agrees with the modern psychologies in that, in the case of desire as in the case of fear, it does not separate the psychic from the somatic. "You will not go after your heart and after your eyes which drag you into infidelity." [6]   "But your eyes and your heart are not but for your covetousness, and for to shed innocent blood, and for oppression, and for violence, to do it." [7]   "Mine eyes languish." [8]   They hope. [9]

Fear is expressed bodily; it is a thing of the body as well as of the mind: "Because of the news that is come, all hearts will melt away, every hand will weaken, every mind will be confused, every knee will melt away to water." [10]   "My loins are filled with anguish." [11]

"So anger, in Hebrew, is expressed in a variety of manners, all equally picturesque, and all borrowed from physiological fact. Metaphors are taken from the rapid and animated breath that escorts passion (אף), * from heat (חרון, חמה) , or boiling (עיר) ; from the action of shattering noisily (רגז) ; from trembling (רעם). Discouragement, despair are expressed as a liquefaction, a dissolving of the heart (מוג מאס, מסה) .   Fear is expressed in the loosening

---

[1] Song of Songs 5: 4.
[2] Jer. 31: 20.
[3] Prov. 23: 16.
[4] Ps. 16: 7.
[5] Ps. 7: 10; Jer. 17: 10 et saepe.
[6] Num. 15: 39.
[7] Jer. 22: 17.
[8] Ps. 119: 123.
[9] Ps. 145: 15.
[10] Ezech. 21: 12.
[11] Is. 21: 3.   On this subject cf. DHORME, *op. cit.* et J. PEDERSEN, *Israël*, I-II, pp. 99-181.

* We have until now transliterated all the quotations in Greek and Hebrew in order to spare the reader who does not know these languages the rather tiresome experience of having to leave a mental blank in the middle of the sentence he is reading.   In this passages, however, we have a series of unvocalized Hebrew radicals which can be of interest only to the Hebrew philologist. A transliteration could only be perplexing to any other reader and so, for once, we have let the Hebrew letters stand. (*Translator's note*)

bearing (נשא ראש, רום, התגבר) . Patience is length of wind (ארך אפים) , impatience a shortness of it (קצר אפים).. Desire is thirst (צמא) , or pallor (כסף) . Forgiveness is expressed by a variety of metaphors taken from the acts of covering, hiding, spreading over a fault the balm that erases it (כסה, כפר) . To shake the head, to look at one another, to let one's arms fall, these are expressions that the Hebrew much prefers to all of our psychological terms, in order to depict disdain, indecision, and discouragement. One may even say that psychological expressions are entirely lacking in Hebrew, or at least that a description of the physical circumstances is added to them: 'he became angry and his face was inflamed,' 'he opened his mouth and said...', etc."

"A distinctive feature of the semitic family of languages is that the primitive union of sensation and idea has always been maintained, that one of the terms has not made them forget the other, as happened in the Aryan languages." [1]

Because he is not a dualist and because he lacks the concept of "body," the Hebrew has a sense, a taste, an intelligence of the carnal. This intelligence is possible only if one does not, after the Manichean fashion, separate the sensible from the intelligible, the body from the soul, in such wise as to deprive the body of significance and render it opaque to intelligence.

No matter how paradoxical it appears to our secretly Manichean habits, the Hebrew has a sense and a love of the carnal because he has a sense of the spiritual and perceives the presence of the spiritual *within* the carnal. The carnal is desirable because of the intelligible mystery with which it is filled. Meaning lies just beneath the skin. The Hebrew is carnal because he knows what is to be learned through the sensible. *

Again because he does not recognize the body-soul dichotomy, the Hebrew can call the union of man and woman a *knowledge (yada)* : "Adam knew Eve, his wife, and she conceived and bore Cain." [2]

"Man was created a living soul." Through love a soul comes to the immediate knowledge of another soul. There is no body

---

[1] RENAN, *Histoire générale et système comparé des langues sémitiques*, pp. 22-24, quoted by M. JOUSSE, *Etudes de psychologie linguistique*, 1925, pp. 44-45.

* We can say as much of a poet like Claudel whose principal intuition is to have found again, beyond the Manichean dualism of Western thought, the biblical understanding of the sensible world's intelligibility, "that which things mean."

[2] Gen. 4: 1; cf. Gen. 4: 17; 19: 8; 24: 16; 38: 26; Judges 19: 25; I Kings 1: 4; Num. 31: 17; Matth. 1: 25; Luke 1: 34.

barrier between them; the body is the soul. The body does not separate, for how can we be separated by what we are? What separates is falsehood. Two living souls learn the "taste" of the other, * the secret taste that is within that name "that no man knows save he that receives it." [1]   This knowledge that lovers acquire of one another is, at the same time, an initiation into the greatest mystery, the subject of the Song of Songs: "I speak concerning Christ and the Church."

"Husbands, love your wives, even as Christ also loved the Church, and gave Himself for it; that He might sanctify and cleanse it with the washing of water by the word, that he might present it to Himself a glorious Church, not having spot, or wrinkle, or any such thing; but that it should be holy and without blemish. So ought men to love their wives as their own bodies. He that loveth his wife loveth himself. For no man ever yet hated his own flesh; but nourisheth and cherisheth it, even as the Lord the Church: for we are members of His body, of His flesh, and of His bones. 'For this cause shall a man leave his father and mother, and shall be joined unto his wife, and they two shall be one flesh.' This is a great mystery: but I speak concerning Christ and the Church." [2]

* * *

Finally the non-dualist structure of biblical anthropology explains certain essential characteristics of biblical language and its

---

* "Il ne connaîtra donc pas ce goût que j'ai?" says DONA PROUHÈZE in *Le Soulier de Satin.*

Claudel, "ab ipsa veritate coactus," led by the inner requirements of poetic reality, clearly felt that the old dualism of body and soul had to be overcome if one was to rediscover the meaning of human love; his poetic intuition led him back to the biblical point of view.

Thus, for instance: "J'ai voulu l'âme, la savoir, cette eau qui ne connaît pas la mort!"

"Car ce n'est pas en aucun autre moment, mais en celui-ci même, que nous posséderons cette femme qui est une seule avec son corps et en qui tout tient ensemble!"

"Qui a goûté le sang (note here, as in Hebrew, the assimilation blood-soul), il ne se nourrira plus d'eau brillante et de miel ardent!"

"Qui a aimé l'âme humaine, qui une fois a été compact avec l'autre âme vivante, il y reste pris pour toujours."

"Quelque chose de lui-même désormais hors de lui vit au pain d'un autre corps." *(Cinq grandes Odes).*

[1] Apoc. 2: 17.
[2] Ephes. 5: 32.

metaphysics. It also explains the pedagogical methods of the
"Rabbis of Israel."

"Though they did not discover its profound anthropological
reason, nor draw the important conclusions the fact implies, the
ancient Palestinian philologists have shown long ago, and quite
correctly, that Hebrew words are actors that play within the text...
What, indeed, are these roots? Simply a transposition upon the
muscles of mouth and larynx of the manual corporal mimes." [1]
"The oral roots of Hebrew and Aramaic are always subtended
by the primordial manual-corporal mimes. In these languages,
style springs from man as a whole and speaks to man as a whole." [2]

Knowledge is not the activity of an intellect set apart from the
body. Semitic man, as Jousse says, is not "dissociated."
Knowledge is an act of the whole man. It is typified in the act
of espousal. "We understand only what we play over again.
Knowledge cannot be a purely passive reception. It is an *action*
that demands of the knower a contribution, and, to this contribution
the depth of his understanding will be proportionate.

* * *

A remark on a pseudo-problem regarding resurrection.

In the New Testament we find the expression: "resurrection
of the dead," *(anastasis nekrōn)*, but not the expression "resurrection
of the body," since neither the idea nor the word are to be found
in Hebrew.

The resurrection of the dead is the resurrection of men. The
Councils, in order to avoid a Platonic interpretation of resurrection,
and to ensure that the "resurrection" of Revelation should not be
confused with the "immortality of the soul" of the Greek
philosophies, felt obliged to specify: *cum corporibus suis*. The
addition was necessary in the circumstances because the biblical
idea was being introduced into a world of dualist thought.
Therefore, to give the full equivalent of what the Bible calls the
resurrection of the dead, they had to specify that this meant the
whole man, that is, in the Greek way of speaking, the soul *and*
the body.

---

[1] M. JOUSSE, *Les Formules targoûmiques du "Pater" dans le milieu ethnique
palestinien*, p. 21.
[2] *Ibid.*, p. 22.

Out of this arose the false problem, how souls could possibly recover the elements of their bodies, after the resurrection, especially if they had been assimilated, directly or otherwise, by other men!

Of course, the problem arises out of an effort to think about the resurrection in terms of a dualist system in which soul and body are two substances. In the context of the Bible, the problem does not exist. Since the soul is the body's essence, since soul and body are but one, the resurrection of bodies is the resurrection of souls that is, the resurrection of men.

The bio-chemical molecules that living man assimilates are quite anonymous. "This skin" and "this eye" are not such or such a molecule of carbon or of water but this very self, this soul that I am, that has assimilated them and informs them from within.

chapter two

A NEW DIMENSION: THE "PNÉUMA"

Hebrew thought spares us the body-soul dichotomy and the array of problems that are peculiar to it. But the biblical tradition reveals, more and more explicitly as revelation progresses, a new element not found in the philosophic anthropologies: the *ruah*. The Septuagint translates this: *pneuma*, and is followed in this by the New Testament.

With the *ruah*, which we call "spirit," biblical anthropology unfolds a new dimension specifically its own. The supernatural dimension is peculiar to revelation. The *pneuma* is in man a supernatural part, a participation in the supernatural order.

If we try to find, in the Greek philosophies, an intuition or presentiment of the spirit in the biblical sense, we may recall what the more contemplative of these philosophers named *theion ti*, something divine, within man. St. Paul hoped to find this point in common with the Athenians: "As certain of your own poets have said: 'We are of his race.' " [1]

According to biblical tradition God's spirit may reside in man. *

Man's spirit, his *pneuma*, is that within him which permits an encounter with the *Pneuma* of God. It is the part of man that can enter into dialogue with God's Spirit, not as a stranger but as a child: "The Spirit itself bears witness with our spirits that we are children of God." [2]

The spirit is, within man, a permanent substantial invitation to a change, to a supernaturalization, that will permit created man to partake of his Creator's uncreated life. Man's *pneuma* is already something supernatural, the "earnest" [3] which admits us to an order

---

[1] Acts 17: 28.
* Cf. Num. 27: 18: "Take Joshua, son of Nun, a man in whom the spirit resides..." Cf. also Num. 11: 17, 25-30; 24: 2; et saepe.
[2] Rom. 8: 16.   [3] 2 Cor. 5: 5.

other than the natural.   The singular characteristic of man in the evolution of living beings is this *passage* from an order of nature to a supernatural order, this participation offered him in his Creator's life, of which participation the spirit is the first-fruits.   It is this which fundamentally distinguishes him from the animal order. This passing-over is an essential aspect of man's nature; we are out of balance in relation to a purely natural state, thrown forward to the spiritual.

"Passage" is the translation of the Hebrew word "pesah," the pasch.   Man is the creature of the pasch, the passage.

The fact is that man never was in a purely natural state * because, it might be said that it is his nature to be a link between the created and the Creator.   The *pneuma* within him is this immaterial bond by which he is raised up to the personal life of God.   In man it is all creation that returns to its Creator: the circle is complete. The physical order has surged forward, lifted by the pulse of life; the psychical order emerged out of the biosphere.   In man it is a truly supernatural order which prepares the consummation of all the created, the fulfilment of the world by its transformation.

Through man the spirit is at work within the world, to bring God's creation to its maturity.

In the full technical sense the Bible gives to the word spirit, we should say that man is a spiritual animal.   Thus was it understood by Claudel: "l'homme et la femme comme deux grands animaux spirituels." [1]

* * *

The flesh-spirit dialectics is proper to the Bible and must not be confused with the body-soul dialectics of the Greeks.   Despite their superficial verbal resemblance these two points of view have nothing in common.   They have been twined together for twenty centuries and we must be very careful to distinguish them in our own minds.

The opposition of flesh to spirit is an opposition between two *orders*.   Flesh, we have seen, is man's index of frailty, that frailty that comes of being made of dust.   The spirit is man's participation in the supernatural order.   The spirit summons

---

* Cf. M. BLONDEL, *Voc. phil.* de Lalande, art. "transnaturel."
[1] CLAUDEL, *Partage de Midi.*

him to the destiny of a god according to what is written: "Ye are gods."

The flesh, we said, is all of man. In Hebrew "flesh" and "soul" are synonyms. "All flesh" and "every soul" mean man or humanity. Hence the spirit-flesh opposition does not mark a duality within nature itself as does the dichotomy of body and soul. It is in fact a distinction between the order of nature and the supernatural which is a revealed order.

From the biblical point of view there is nothing spiritual in an ethics that exalts the soul at the expense of the body. Such philosophies are carnal. Indeed the more they exalt the soul the more carnal they are. They contribute, says St. Paul, to "the satisfaction of the flesh." [1] An asceticism that represses the "body" is at least as carnal as Epicurianism. *

In the Old Testament as in the New it is often difficult to tell whether there is question of the *ruah*, the *pneuma* of God, or of the pneuma of man. This difficulty is significant: the spirit within man is a participation. The inhabitation of man by God's Spirit is made possible by the existence of a spirit in man.

In any case spirit is constitutive of man's very existence. "As long as... the *ruah* of God is in my nostrils..." [2] "My spirit will not always remain in man, for man is but flesh." [3] "You take away their breath *(ruah)*, they die and return to dust." [4]

When death comes: "The dust returns to the earth as it was, and the spirit — *ruah* — returns unto God who gave it." [5] "If He gathers unto Himself His spirit *(ruah)* and His breath *(nischemat)* all flesh shall perish together and man shall turn again unto dust." [6] God is called "the God of the spirits of all flesh." [7]

Man, alone before his Creator, is essentially weak. "The Egyptians are men and not God, and their horses flesh and not

---

[1] Col. 2: 23.

* "Nam qui velut summum bonum laudat animae naturam, et tanquam malum naturam carnis accusat, profecto et animam carnaliter appetit, et carnem carnaliter fugit: quoniam id vanitate sentit humana, non veritate divina." (Anyone that praises the soul as the greatest good and blames the flesh as evil clearly both seeks the soul and flees the flesh in a carnal manner. For such judgments are those of human vanity, not of divine Truth.) St. Augustine, *De civitate Dei*, 14: 5.

[2] Job 27: 3.   [3] Gen. 6: 3.
[4] Ps. 104: 29.   [5] Eccl. 12: 7.
[6] Job 34: 14.   [7] Num. 16: 22; 27: 16.

spirit." [1]   "What can flesh (lit.: a flesh) do unto me?" [2]   "He remembered that they were but flesh." [3]

In the New Testament we find this same idea of a natural "asthenia," a weakness, natural in man because he is flesh: "the *pneuma* is willing, but the flesh is weak *(asthenēs)*." [4]   *("Astheneia tes sarkos")*. [5]   Here as in the Old Testament it is the spirit that gives life: "It is the spirit that quickens, the flesh can be of no use here." *

If we live only within the biological order without participating in the spirit that calls us to a new destiny, then we shall die like all that is biological, without having set foot in the imperishable order: "for if you live according to the flesh, you shall die." [6]   "Flesh and blood *(sarx kai aima,* cf. Hebrew: *basār wedam)* cannot inherit the kingdom of God, neither does corruption inherit incorruption. Behold I show you a mystery: we shall not all sleep, but we shall all be changed." [7]

As we have pointed out, the spirit is, in man, a call to transformation.   According to certain texts of St. Paul it would appear that, even without the accident of an original "fall," God's original plan entailed a transformation that was to raise the biological beings that we are to a superior and final state.   We cannot pass from one order to another without undergoing this transformation which, as a consequence of sin, has become for us as difficult and painful as birth itself.   In sorrow we are brought forth to the supernatural life.   "That which is born of the flesh is flesh, and that which is born of the spirit is spirit.   Do not be surprised that I told you: you must be born from above.   The wind *(pneuma)* blows as it wills and you hear its voice, but you cannot tell where it comes from, nor where it goes: so is it with everyone that is born of the spirit." [8]

There are a "will of the flesh," a mind, affections, and desires of the flesh, ** all opposed to those of the spirit. The "works of

---

[1] Is. 31: 3.
[2] Ps. 56: 5.
[3] Ps. 78: 39.
[4] Matth. 36: 41.
[5] Gal. 4: 13; cf. Rom. 8: 3.
* John 6: 63.
[6] Rom. 8: 13.
[7] I Cor. 15: 50.
[8] John 3: 6 et sq.

** It is pointed out by O. Procksch (*Theologie des Alten Testament*, p. 460) that we find in the Bible the expression "spirit of life," *ruaḥ ḥajjim* but never the expression "living spirit."   Contrariwise we never find "soul of life," but only "living soul," *nephesch hajja*.   The soul is the substance into which the spirit comes.

the flesh" are not only, as in a dualist context, "fornication, impurity, sensuality," but also (and this would be absurd if body and soul were not one), "idolatry, recourse to witchcraft, hatred, quarreling, jealousy, bad temper, rivalry, factions, heresies, envy." [1] St. Augustine notes the incompatibility of the familiar Manichean opposition of body to soul with this new distinction of the psychological and the spiritual order: "in operibus namque carnis... non illa tantum invenimus, quae ad voluptatem pertinent carnis, sicut fornicationes, etc., verum etiam illa quibus animi vitia demonstrantur a voluptate carnis aliena. Quis enim servitutem quae idolis exhibetur, veneficia, inimicitias, contentiones, aemulationes, animositates, dissentiones, haereses, invidias, non potius intelligat animi esse vitia quam carnis?" [*]   In all these texts we see that "flesh" is not what Plato called "the body," but is man, "a living soul."

* *
*

The distinction between the spiritual and the carnal is identical with that between the spiritual and the psychological. For, as we have seen, "flesh" and "soul" both stand for natural man.

"The word of God is living, it is powerful, sharper than any two-edged sword; so penetrating as to separate the soul from the spirit *(achri merismou psuchēs kai pneumatos.)*" [2] "Thus the raising of the dead... it is sown a 'psychical' body *(sōma psuchikon)*, it is raised a spiritual body *(sōma pneumatikon)*. There is a psychical body and there is a spiritual body. And so it is written: the first man Adam was made a living soul *(eis psuchēn zōsan)*; the last Adam was made a life-giving spirit *(eis pneuma zōopoioun)*. However, the spiritual order does not come first, but the psychical *(ou prōton to pneumatikon alla to psuchikon)* and only afterwards

---

[1] John 1: 13; Col. 2: 18; Rom. 8: 6 respectively.
[*] *De Civitate Dei*, 14: 2. "For among the works of the flesh... we find not only those which concern the pleasure of the flesh, as fornications, uncleanness, lasciviousness, drunkenness, revellings, but also those which, though they be remote from fleshly pleasure, reveal the vices of the soul. For who does not see that idolatries, witchcrafts, hatreds, variance, emulations, wrath, strife, heresies, envyings, are vices rather of the soul than of the flesh?" (the English from the Marcus Dods translation published by the Modern Library, N. Y.).
[2] Hebr. 4: 12.

the spiritual. The first man was of earth, made of dust; the second man came from heaven." *

"The spirit sees all things, even the depths of God. For what man knows the things of man save the spirit of man which is within him? So too the things of God no man knows but the spirit of God. As to ourselves, it is not the spirit of the world that we have received, but the spirit of God, that we might know the things that God has given us. Things that we speak of, not in the words of human wisdom, but in the words of the spirit, showing the accord of spiritual things for those that are spiritual *(pneumatikois)*. Now as to psychical man *(psuchikos anthrōpos)* he does not perceive those things that are of the spirit of God; to him they appear ridiculous, and he cannot know them for it is spiritually *(pneumatikōs)* that one judges them." [1]

"If you have in your hearts a bitter zeal and a quarrelsome spirit, do not glorify yourselves and do not lie against truth: it is not such a wisdom that comes from above: it is earthly, psychical *(psuchikē)*, devilish." [2] "Psychical, not having the spirit *(psuchikoi, pneuma mē echontes)*." [3]

"*Psuchikos*" in all these texts is exactly synonymous of "*sarkikos*," fleshly.

This distinction between the psychological and the spiritual order is of capital importance: it is the key to the Christian theology of the supernatural. And while it is identical with the distinction between carnal and spiritual it has the advantage of avoiding any possible confusion with the Platonic dualism of body and soul.

Now whenever this confusion *has* occured it has had two consequences, which are correlative:

(1) the biblical dialectics of man and his supernatural vocation (its germ: the spirit) is reduced to a more or less Manichean type

---

* I Cor. 15, 42. We find, in the writings of Paul, the idea of a progressive *plan*, of an "economy" in the genesis of man.   First the creation of man as we know him, a spiritual animal inheriting from the biological order his frailty and his caducity. Then a transformation of "animal," psychical, man into a spiritual (pneumatikos) man.   "For flesh and blood cannot inherit the kingdom of God, nor can corruption inherit the incorruptible (1 Cor. 15, 50). The corruptible must put on incorruptibility.   It seems that, even without the appearance of original sin, a transformation was intended by God to lift man from a lower condition to plenitude.   But instead of being painful and passing through the tormented a state of mediation of death, this transformation would have been an "assumption" which would have transfigured this earthly body into a "glorious body."

[1] I Cor. 2: 10-15.
[2] James 3: 14.   [3] Jude 19.

of Platonic dualism.   Consequently Christianity is reduced to a kind of moralism, to a form of asceticism.   There is no greater misconstruction of the essence of Christianity.

(2) the exact and specifically supernatural meaning of *pneuma* in biblical revelation is ignored, and thus the sense and original dimension of Christian spirituality is lost.

These two confusions are linked.   The reduction of Christianity to a Manichean form of moralism and the loss of the sense of the supernatural are always allied in the history of heresies.

* * *

The theological virtues of faith, hope, and charity (which properly belong to Christian theology founded on Revelation), are not *psychological* but *spiritual*.   They are of the order of the *pneuma* and not of that of the *psyche (= sarx)*.   And because they are supernatural they cannot be the object of a psychological analysis. Such an analysis can indeed make an inventory of all that the spiritual is *not* and in this sense it is valuable, especially if it penetrates into the unconscious, because it *liberates* the spiritual, in the sense in which it is said that photography liberated painting.   Psychology fulfils a cathartic function in relation to the supernatural order. Positive knowledge of one order will show us how far it extends and where another order begins.   Thus psychological analysis helps us untangle the spiritual from all that it is not.

Faith is a theological virtue.   It should not be confused with *belief* which can be psychologically understood.   A psychological analysis can cover the whole psychological context of faith.   Its subject is everything that faith is not: the affective, sometimes infantile elements surrounding it, the unconscious conflicts. But faith itself is a spiritual intelligence, *sunesis pneumatikē*, [1] a supernatural understanding that the spirit gives us.

Charity is neither affective love, nor a kind of philanthropy that can be explained by psychological motives or by temperament. Neither affection, nor sentiment, nor passion, charity is of another order: the spiritual, the supernatural.

Hope has nothing in common with natural optimism.   It is not an easy hopefulness, companion to a fortunate temperament.   Hope too is a supernatural virtue which can subsist beyond all wrecks

---

[1] Col. I: 9.

and beyond all human dereliction. It is that voice rising from the pit of *human* despair: "Out of the depths have I cried unto Thee, O Lord." Only here, in the despair of nature, is hope to be measured.

The great Christian spiritual authors were not mistaken on this point. The distinction between the psychological (the carnal) and the spiritual is the foundation of any authentically Christian mystic life. The entire work of St. John of the Cross, for instance, is an effort to make this distinction between the affective, that which is of the soul, and the spirit conversing with the Spirit of God.

* * *

In biblical anthropology love between man and woman appears in a perspective that ties it to a love greater than itself. Two living souls who know one another, and who live their life out of the intuition that each has of the other, are by the same token initiated into the mystery of the Song of Songs.

How shall we understand the beauty of the human face if it is not the glow of that fire consuming man from within, the earnest of the spirit, the first-fruits of a supernatural destiny, the fire of the *pneuma* summoning him to such a transmutation as will make a god of him. For man's beauty is the beauty of a god, a sorrowful god or a god inwardly burned by fire. "We have this treasure in earthen vessels."

Beauty is a "resemblance." [1] Sometimes, looking at certain faces one has an inkling of what the spiritual body will be once the inner beauty has consumed the outer bark.

---

[1] Gen. I: 26.

Part three

UNDERSTANDING

"I am understanding,
I have strength."
(Prov. 8 : 14)

chapter one

THE HEART OF MAN

"I sleep but my heart waketh."

The biblical metaphysics of being is original in that it considers reality as created.

Biblical psychology is original in that it considers man's thoughts as *created* by man, generated by his freedom within his heart. Man is the creator of his thoughts; he is their responsible author.

We find in the Bible an entire psychology of the secret source in man of his original freedom and of the genesis of thoughts out of an original choice that is the root of all our reasonings. There is no double ledger in man's mind, no sealed partition between thought and liberty, that first and essential act which determines a being. The play of thought does not go on in some pure region, separate from the initial option of the heart and from its obscure designs. The opposite of truth is not error but falsehood. There is falsehood and not mere error, because in the secret depths of man truth lives and is at work upon him. Truth opens a dialogue between itself and man, a dialogue that is the moral conscience. But man can repress and hide from his own eyes the demands of truth within him; thereafter man is split; his heart is split. The inner contradictions thus brought on can lead a man even to madness. Certain texts suggest this explanation of the genesis of madness.

* * *

Seen in an evolutionary perspective, in other words seen in time, God's creative action till the appearance of man seems to have worked in the darkness of organic life. There, biological evolution, rising like a flare, unfolded its vast ramification of species. Ever more elaborate species, ever more complex organisms, ever more mobile animals with ever more perfect nervous systems — all these were unfolded with the surety of an act that in no way depends on the individuals thus progressively engendered. Nothing was required of the individual. He was a transition, a step, a springboard for an action that surpassed him. The wisdom inherent in animal instinct seems a wisdom of unawakened beings.

But in man, for the first time, the creative action becomes conscious, not only in itself, but for the beings it engenders. It can now be reflected upon by them. Henceforth the creative action depends upon them in a certain way. The creative action has recruited collaborators. History is a work in which divine action and human action cooperate. *"Theou gar esmen sunergoi,* we are co-workers of God." At the peak of the universe, like the flower of the Creative act that made the world and life, mankind to a certain extent holds in its power the fulfilment of the creative gesture. Mankind can halt the movement, reverse it, or carry it to its fulfilment, to its *plerōma*. This choice is man's because he is *conscious*. With intelligence comes risk. Man became like God, says the book of Genesis, knowing what is good and bad, both for himself and for the destiny of the whole *Magnum Opus.* So ended the realm of the immanent and unfailing wisdom that operates with the beauty and assurance we see in animals. Man can stand apart from this immanent wisdom. He can look at it and distinguish himself from it. Man has the power to reverse creative action in himself. But he can also pursue it in the direction of which he is conscious. It is this awareness of the creative action of God in man that St. Paul calls the *suneidēsis,* the spiritual intelligence. Because it is at work within us we are aware of that action that brought us into being and that strives to continue its work within us, and with us. Of course we can hide its demands from our sight, we can stand up against them, we can, up to a point, deny this Will that works on us, a will more primitive and intimate than our own, but we cannot abolish it. A sincere examination will always uncover it beneath the contradictions of our thoughts and actions. The problem, says Blondel, "is to find out whether... in the depths of the unconscious life whence the mystery of action emerges like an enigma whose answer may well be terrible, whether I say, among all the wanderings of mind and heart, the seed of a science and the principle of an intimate revelation do not nevertheless subsist; a seed and principle such that once we have them, nothing will appear arbitrary or unaccountable within the destiny of each person... Therefore must we ask, is there not at the root of the most impertinent negations and the most foolhardy extravagances of the will, an initial movement that always persists, that one loves and wills even when one denies it or abuses it." [1] "Recapture... the truth that is essential to every conscience, the movement that is common to all wills." "Taking into ourselves all consciences we must become the intimate accomplice of every one, in order to discover whether they carry in themselves their justification or their condemnation. Let them be their own judges. Let them see where their will would lead them in its greatest sincerity and its most intimate reality. Let them learn what they do without knowing, and what they know already without wanting and without doing." [2] "To reveal the most intimate orientation of each heart, even to the primitive movement's final accord or contradiction with the end it reaches, it should suffice that will and action be allowed to unfold in every one." *

* * *

"Heart" in the Bible does not, as in our Western tradition, mean the affections, sensibility as opposed to reason. It is rather man's liberty, the centre in which are taken the fundamental decisions; in particular the choices between knowledge and ignorance, light and darkness, understanding and what the prophets call stupidity, foolishness. In the "heart" the strife unfolds what will decide man's destiny, his very essence: according to the essence he has chosen, man will be judged. For man chooses himself as he wills to be and this is the justification of the judgment upon him.

The matter of judgment is this intimate *orientation* of the heart, and not the degrees of accomplishment that men may appraise. This basic choice escapes observation by others and sometimes indeed escapes the subject's eye: in this case we have bad faith. The subject effectively obscures the matter so as not to see into it himself. Sartre's analyses of bad faith have a certain affinity with biblical psychology.

The obscurity of the secret debate, whose essential decisions shape each man's destiny, does not reduce the subject's responsibility. A conscience mystified, the bad conscience of bad faith,

---

[1] M. BLONDEL, *L'Action*, 1893, p. xx.
[2] *Id.*, p. xxi.
* *Id.*, p. xxii. Cf. too p. xxiv, p. xxv. Blondel rediscovered a metaphysics of mind and action which is that of the Bible.

is responsible conscience nonetheless.   And though man cannot fathom the heart's secret designs, God can, and God judges them.

"The heart is deceitful above all things, and corrupt; who can know it?   I, Yhwh, who search the hearts and try the reins." [1] "Yhwh tries the reins and hearts." [2]   "Try in the furnace my reins and my heart." [3]   "God... knows the secrets of the heart" *(ta krupta tēs kardias).* [4]

"Therefore judge nothing before the time, until the Lord come: he will bring to light the things hidden in darkness *(ta krupta tou skotous),* and will make manifest the counsels of the hearts *(kai fanerōsei tas boulas tōn kardiōn).* [5]

"Thus are the secrets of his heart made manifest," *(ta krupta tēs kardias autou fanera ginetai).* [6]

"For the word of God is living, it is powerful, sharper than any two-edged sword... a discerner of the sentiments and thoughts of the heart" *(kritikos enthumēseōn kai ennoiōn kardias).* [7]

"There is nothing hidden that shall not be revealed, and nothing secret *(krupton)* that shall not be known." [8]

This doctrine of the heart's secret will implies the idea of the heart's *duplicity:*

"Each one speaks lies to his neighbor; with flattering lips and with a double heart *(beleb weleb,* LXX: *en kardia kai en kardia)* do they speak." [9]   James speaks of "double-minded man," *(dipsuchos).* [10]   And the Psalmist asks: "Lord, unite my heart." [11]

An old text clarifies this psychology of the heart's secrets and its duplicity.   As Cain is jealous of his brother, and as the desire to kill him grows — in the secret of his heart, "Yhwh said to Cain: Why are you angry and why is your countenance fallen?   If you do well, will you not be accepted?   And if you do not well, does not sin lie at your door?   Its desire shall turn towards you, but you must rule over it." [12]

The word used for "sin" in Hebrew is in the feminine gender. This expression "Its desire shall turn towards you" is the same

---

[1] Jer. 17: 9, 10.
[2] Jer. 11: 20; 20: 12; Ps. 7: 10 ff.
[3] Ps. 26: 2.
[4] Ps. 44: 22.
[5] 1 Cor. 4: 5.
[6] 1 Cor. 14: 25.
[7] Heb. 4: 12.
[8] Luke 12: 2.
[9] Ps. 12: 3.
[10] Cf. James 1: 8; 4: 8.
[11] Ps. 86: 11; cf. Col. 3: 22.
[12] Gen. 4: 6, 7.

as in Genesis 3: 16, where woman is told: "Your desire shall be unto your husband, and he shall rule over you." [1]

The picture evoked by the first text on sin is that of a bitch lying down on the doorstep. The essential idea is that there is a duality between sin and man, a spontaneity proper to sin that introduces a duality into man. If man recognizes this duality and rules over that portion of himself that, in a way leads its own life, the conflict can remain well defined and healthy. But if instead, by half opening the door he lets the bitch at his doorstep into the house without knowing it, he will become double. In the depths of his heart begins a dance. Man becomes a stranger to himself, *alienated*.

Thoughts *arise* in the heart (*'alah 'al leb*) out of an original freedom that engenders them.

"Thoughts will arise in your heart and you will conceive an evil plan." [2] "This I commanded not, nor spake it, nor did it arise in my heart.' [3]

In the New Testament we find the same idea:

"Why do thoughts arise in your heart. [4] "It came into his heart to visit his brothers." [5] "The thoughts of your heart," (*hē epinoia tēs kardias sou*). [6]

"It is not what goes into the mouth that defiles a man, but what comes out of the mouth, this defiles a man." [7] "The mouth speaks out of the abundance of the heart." [8] "What comes out of the mouth comes from the heart, and this defiles a man. For out of the heart come all evil thoughts (*dialogismoi ponēroi*), murders, adulteries, fornications, thefts, false witnesses, blasphemies." [9] "From within, out of the heart, come evil thoughts, fornications, thefts, murders, adulteries, avariciousness, wickedness, deceit, lasciviousness, envy, blasphemy, pride (*huperēphania*), folly (*aphrosunē*)." [10]

In both texts the enumerations begin with "evil thoughts." "Why do thoughts arise in your hearts?" [11] "Why do you think evil in your hearts?" (*hinati enthumeisthe ponēra en tais kardiais humōn*). [12] "They were reasoning in their hearts," (*dialogezomenoi*

---

[1] Gen. 3: 16.
[2] Ez. 38: 10.
[3] Jer. 19: 5; cf. 7: 31; 32: 35; Is. 65: 17.
[4] Luke 24: 38.
[5] Acts 7: 23.
[6] Acts 8: 22.
[7] Matth. 15: 11; cf. Mark 7: 15.
[8] Matth. 12: 34.
[9] Matth. 15: 18, 19.
[10] Mark 7: 21.
[11] Luke 24: 38.
[11] Matth. 9: 4.

en tais kardiais). [1] "Why do you reason these things in your hearts?" *(ti tauta dialogizesthe en tais kardiais humōn).* [2]

Mark's enumeration ends with pride and folly.

⋆ ⋆ ⋆

Understanding is an act that proceeds from the freedom of the heart. Stupidity also proceeds from this original freedom. "They have made their hearts as hard as a diamond in order not to hear." [3] "Their heart is as insensible as fat." [4] "You men, stiff-necked and uncircumcised in heart and ears, you always resist the Holy Spirit." [5] "They had not understood... for their heart had become calloused *(pepōrōmenē).*" [6] "Do you not yet perceive, have you no understanding?   Has your heart become hard?" [7]

The *pōrōsis* is a callous growth: "their understanding is obscured by the *pōrōsis* of their heart." [8] "I will rend the caul of their heart." [9] "Circumcise the foreskin of your heart." [10] "Yhwh your God will circumcise your heart." [11] "Circumcise yourselves for Yhwh and take away the foreskin of your heart." [12]

Yhwh even breaks hearts as one breaks a clump of dry earth that it may receive the rain and the seed. "When I have broken their whorish heart... they will know that I am Yhwh." [13] "Yhwh is near to them that have a broken heart." [14] "Rend your hearts and not your garments." [15]

"And I will give you a new heart, and I will put a new spirit within you; I will take away the heart of stone out of your flesh, and I will give you a heart of flesh.   And I will put My spirit within you." [16]

Understanding is an action, the result of a choice, of a fundamental disposition; it is born in the secret recesses of the heart. "Who is the man who would dispose his heart to approach unto me?" [17]

"Fear not, Daniel, from the first day that you set your heart to understand, and to humble yourself before God, your words were heard." [18]

---

[1] Mark 2: 6.
[3] Zach. 7: 12.
[5] Acts 7: 51.
[7] Mark 8: 17.
[9] Hos. 13: 8.
[11] Deut. 30: 6.
[13] Ez. 6: 9, 10.
[15] Joel 2: 13.
[17] Jer. 30: 21.

[2] Mark 2: 8.
[4] Ps. 119: 70.
[6] Mark 6: 52.
[8] Eph. 4: 18.
[10] Deut. 10: 16.
[12] Jer. 4: 4.
[14] Ps. 34: 18.
[16] Ez. 36: 26.
[18] Dan. 10: 12.

Lack of understanding also comes from a secret choice, a choice of the personality at its deepest point. Understanding is a virtue, stupidity is sin. *Stultitia est peccatum.* Stupidity too is an action. "They became vain in their thoughts and their foolish hearts were darkened." [1]

The heart is that original freedom from which understanding and knowledge proceed. "Yet Yhwh has not given you a heart that understands, eyes that see, ears that hear, to this day." [2] "I will give them a heart to know me, that I am Yhwh." [3] "Make you a new heart and a new spirit." [4]

Stupidity is an act of hardening, of shutting. "You have shut their hearts to understanding." [5] "The Lord opened her heart that she attend to what Paul said." [6]

And it is in the heart, in its secret depths, at freedom's spring that the *pneuma* of God comes. "God has given us the earnest of the spirit in our hearts." [7] "God has sent forth the spirit of His Son into our hearts." [8] "That the Father of glory may give you a spirit of wisdom and of revelation to know him, and that he may enlighten the eyes of your heart" *(pephōtismenous tous ophthalmous tēs kardias).* [9]

Understanding does not consist in judging but in listening. It is, in Bergson's words, a "spiritual auscultation."

"Hear, O Israel... you shall love Yhwh your God with your whole heart." [10] Mark translates this correctly in Greek: with your whole mind, with your whole understanding" *(ex holēs tēs dianoias, ex holēs tēs suneseōs).* [11]

"The Lord has opened my ear." [12] "Morning by morning he wakens my ear that I may listen as a disciple." [13] "Does not the ear try words?" [14] "And the ears of all the people were to the book of the Tora." [15] Here as with the heart, lack of understanding is a hardness: "their ears are uncircumcised." [16]

Understanding means listening. Hence the importance of silence: "Be silent Israel, and listen." [17]

---

[1] Rom. 1: 21.
[2] Deut. 29: 4.
[3] Jer. 24: 7.
[4] Ez. 18: 31.
[5] Job 17: 4.
[6] Acts 16: 14.
[7] 2 Cor. 1: 22.
[8] Gal. 4: 6.
[9] Ephes. 1: 17.
[10] Deut. 6: 5.
[11] Mark 12: 29, 33.
[12] Is. 50: 5.
[13] *Ibid.*, 4.
[14] Job 12: 11.
[15] Neh. 8: 3.
[16] Jer. 6: 10.
[17] Deut. 27: 9.

"In Gibeon Yhwh appeared to Solomon in a dream by night, and God said: Ask what I shall give you... Solomon answered... give to your servant a listening heart *(leb schōme'a)* * to judge your people with understanding. That I may distinguish between good and evil.

"And God said: because you have asked understanding to discern justice, ** behold I give you a wise and understanding heart, so that there was none like you before you, neither after you shall anyone arise like unto you." [1]

---

* LXX: *kardian akouein ... tou sunein.*
** LXX: *sunesin tou eisakouein krima.*
[1] 1 Kings 3: 5-14.

chapter two

MIND AND ACTION

"There is nothing in Hebrew that corresponds to *nous*. The word *nous* itself is rare even in the LXX where, most often, it is a translation of *leb*, heart, ★ and appears rather to express the translator's own culture. It appears somewhat more frequently during the Hellenistic period. But it is lacking in the Gospels, save once in that of the Hellenist Luke (24: 45). To express 'understanding,' as in the Old Testament, the evangelists use *kardia* (*leb*, heart)." ★★

What the prophets call understanding, *bina*, is not a faculty, an *organon* endowed with certain *a priori* categories, a power that would pass into action under certain circumstances. Understanding *is* action, the act of intellection of subsistent truth. Hebrew, a concrete language, never speaks of understanding except in such a context of truth's fruition. It names understanding only when it is in action, an understanding of its proper object.

Understanding is a dialogue, an existential relation of two liberties, that of God and that of man, an exchange in which God gives man understanding to know the " secrets of the King. " Understanding is a circulation from I to THOU. Aside from this flow there is no understanding. Understanding is this movement with two points of departure, each source being liberty. God's is called grace.

Man asks for understanding: "Give me understanding." [1] "Give me understanding according to your word." [2] "Give me under-

---

★ Ex. 7: 23; Jud. 8: 14; Is, 10: 7, 12; 41: 22; Job 7: 17, 20; 1 Esd. 2: 9; 9: 41.
★★ Matth. 13: 15; 15: 19; Luke 2: 35; 24: 15, 38; Acts 8: 22; 28: 27; John 12: 40; Mark 2: 6, 8; 3: 5; 6: 52; 8: 17. FESTUGIERE, *L'idéal religieux des Grecs et l'évangile*, p. 208, footnote.
[1] Ps. 119: 125.   [2] *Ibid.*, 169.

standing that I may live." [1]   Solomon asks: "Grant me understanding and wisdom." [2]

God gives understanding, gave it in the beginning when He made man: "God gives us understanding, more than to the fowls of heaven." [3]   He gives it now under a new economy: "For Yhwh gives wisdom, out of His mouth comes knowledge and under-standing." [4]   Thus also in the New Testament: "The Lord give you understanding in all things," [5] "He has given us understanding that we may know the truth." [6]

This relation between God and man that is understanding is established through the inhabitation within man of a supernatural element, *ruaḥ*, the *pneuma:* "It is a spirit in man, and an inspiration of the Almighty that gives understanding." [7] "I have filled him with the spirit of God, in wisdom, and in understanding, and in knowledge, and in all manner of workmanship." [8]

The biblical conception of understanding is tied to its anthropology, and particularly to its doctrine of the *pneuma.* Understanding, in the Bible, is a "spiritual intelligence," *sunesis pneumatikē.* [9]

* * *

Understanding is not apart from life, life is not dissociated from intelligence. They are inseparably linked: "Give me understanding that I may live." [10]

Knowledge is not a luxury nor a useless epiphenomenon. It is a question of life or death: "My people are destroyed for lack of knowledge; because you have rejected knowledge I will also reject you: you shall be no priest to me." [11]

Knowledge and life are but One: "The life was the light of men." [12] "This is the life eternal, that they may know You, the only God." [13]

Progress in knowledge is the road to life: "You will make known to me the path of life." [14]

---

[1] *Ibid.*, 144.
[2] Chron. 1: 10; 1 Kings 3: 9.
[3] Job 35: 11.
[4] Prov. 2: 6.
[5] 2 Tim. 2: 7.
[6] 1 John 5: 20.
[7] Job 32: 8.
[8] Ex. 31: 3.
[9] Col. 1: 9.
[10] Ps. 119: 144.
[11] Hos. 4: 6.
[12] John 1: 4.
[13] John 17: 3.
[14] Ps. 16: 11.

Loss of knowledge is death: "This I say therefore... that you henceforth walk not as the Gentiles walk in the vanity of their intellect; their understanding is darkened and they are strangers to the life of God, through the ignorance that is in them, because of the *sclerosis* of their heart." [1]

Understanding is not separate from action. It is an action that demands the participation of the whole of man. Proceeding from man's heart it is the act of his inmost liberty, and cannot be distinguished from the practical dispositions of the heart that does the choosing. Understanding depends on an innermost choice, the fundamental choice of the man. It is the essential act that defines and judges him, being elaborated by all his inner powers, both conscious and unconscious. No double ledger can be kept with action on one side, thought on the other. Thought is not in itself "pure," not set in a place apart, *topos noetos*.

Understanding is inseparable from the good. "To depart from evil is understanding." [2] "When wisdom enters into your heart and knowledge is pleasant to your soul, reflection will watch over you, understanding will keep you, to deliver you from the way of evil." [3]

Understanding is our most important act. We are responsible for it. Understanding, in the Old Testament as in the New, is the foremost value. It is a virtue, the prime virtue from which all the others proceed: "Let him that glories glory in this: that he has understanding and that he knows Me." [4]

Knowledge is the prime virtue: "We know thee, (we), Israel." [5] "Let us apply ourselves to knowing Yhwh." [6] "Continue your kindness to those that know you and your justice to the upright in heart." [7] "Pour out your wrath upon the nations that have not known you." [8]

The greatest blame that God lays on His people by the mouth of His prophets, is that they allow knowledge to be lost. "For my people is mad, they do not know me, they are senseless sons that have no understanding." [9] "There is no truth nor mercy nor knowledge of God in the land." [10] "For I desire the knowledge of God more than burnt offerings." [11]

---

[1] Eph. 4: 18.
[3] Prov. 2: 10.
[5] Hos. 8: 3.
[7] Ps. 36: 10.
[9] Jer. 4: 22.
[11] Hos. 6: 6.

[2] Job 28: 28.
[4] Jer. 9: 23.
[6] Hos. 6: 3.
[8] Ps. 79: 6.
[10] Hos. 4: 1.

And in the New Testament: "The world knew Him not." [1] "Righteous Father, the world has not known You." [2]

Lack of knowledge, unintelligence is a sin. It is *the* sin.

Knowledge of God is not purely speculative but an action incarnated in the world of men: "He did judgment and justice... he judged the cause of the poor and the needy.... Is not this to know me? Word of Yhwh." [3]

Nothing is more contrary to the biblical conception of knowledge and understanding than a separation of thought and action. In the words of Marx: "The philosophers have merely interpreted the world in different ways: the important thing is to transform it."

Understanding and knowledge, according to the Bible, are an action that requires the whole of man. Knowledge of God is not at all an evasion out of this world in the Platonic manner; in fact it cannot be separated from concrete action: "By this do we know that we know Him: if we keep His commandments." [4] "Whoever sins has not seen Him and does not know Him." He that says: "I know Him, and keeps not His commandments is a liar." [5]

Understanding is holiness: "The knowledge of the holy is understanding." [6]

The messianic era is that of the knowledge of Yhwh: "A man shall no more teach his neighbor, nor a man his brother, saying: know Yhwh. For they shall all know me." [7] "The earth shall be full of the knowledge of Yhwh, as the waters cover the sea." *

The good is not separate from life.

"I made them go out of the land of Egypt and brought them into the wilderness. I gave them my statutes and showed them my judgments, which if a man do he shall have life." [8] "If he

---

[1] John 1: 10.
[2] John 17: 25; cf. John 15: 21; Rom. 1: 28; 1 Cor. 15: 34; Gal. 4: 8, etc.
[3] Jer. 22: 16.   [4] 1 John 2: 3.
[5] *Ibid.*   [6] Prov. 9: 10.
[7] Jer. 31: 34.
* Is. 11, 9. The knowledge man acquires of God proceeds from the knowledge God has of man. These two are one. The verb *yada* means both to know and to marry. Woman knows man because he knows her. The knowledge between Yhwh and the "virgin of Israel" is analogous: "in the wilderness I knew you" (Hos. 13: 5; cf. Ez. 16). "Before I formed you in the belly I knew you" (Jer. 1: 5). "I called you by your name, I appointed you when you knew me not" (Is. 45: 4). Cf. Rom. 8: 29. "Whoever loves God he is known by him" (1 Cor. 8: 3 and 1 Cor. 13: 12).
[8] Ez. 20: 10.

keeps the statutes of life... he shall live." "See I have set before you this day life and good, and death and evil." [1] "Behold I set before the way of life and the way of death." [2]

"Choose life that you may live, you and your seed, that you may love Yhwh your God, that you may obey His voice and that you may cleave unto him: for He is your life." [3]

Understanding is not separate from good, nor is good separate from Yhwh. There is no moral system aside from the theological metaphysics oriented on Yhwh.

Biblical thought contains nothing comparable to what philosophical thought calls "ethics." This may, at first sight, seem paradoxical. The Bible's specific contribution has too often been represented as a more perfected and more human moral doctrine. But such a representation is the reduction of one world — that of the prophets of Israel — to another — that of the Western philosophers — and a fundamental error concerning the originality of the Judeo-Christian contribution. To reduce this contribution to an "ethics" is in fact nothing less than a betrayal.

Those biblical concepts that appear analogous to our notions of ethics really have a quite different significance. This is because they belong to an entirely different system of references. They are, as the physicist would say, in an absolutely new "field." These concepts find their meaning in a world that gravitates about Him whose Name is *I am*. They are integrated into a metaphysics and a theology and cannot be separated from them without losing their substance. To consider separately the concepts of an "ethics" of the Old or New Testament is a fatal mistake for anyone that wants to understand their true scope. Such a separation leaves a mere corruptible residue which rots like manna, because it is being preserved apart from the whole that produced it. *

Thus justice in the Bible (the *Zedaka*) has not only, nor primarily, an ethical or a social significance. The Zedaka is the justice, or the justness, of our essential metaphysical relationship with God. This

---

[1] Deut. 30: 15; cf. 30: 6, 19; 33: 47.

[2] Jer. 21: 8.   [3] Deut. 30: 20.

* "The fundamental notions of philosophical ethics are lacking in the New Testament. They are either completely lacking as in the case of *eudaimonia*, or they appear very rarely, like *aretē* in the epistles of St. Peter and (only once) in the epistles of St. Paul, or again they acquire a new, religious meaning like *dikaiosunē*, a justice that has value in the eyes of God. Conversely, *agapē* which is so essential to Christianity is unknown in pagan thought, even as a word." POHLENS, *Die Stoa*, p. 406.

precise relationship is knowledge and love. Justice in the Bible is not opposed to charity. It *is* charity. The theological virtue of justice expresses itself in justice towards neighbor, which is also love, and in social justice.

So we must avoid thinking of this term of Justice in the restricted legal sense we give it in the Western world. Biblical justice is primarily theological.

If we wish to place the biblical metaphysics of understanding in relation to its exact opposite, we must turn to Kant. Kantism is really the reverse of the biblical point of view. And that which is one in the Bible is separate and dissociated in Kantian doctrine: knowledge and being, virtue and understanding, virtue and the fulness of being, life. From the biblical point of view the Kantian dichotomies break into ineffective fragments something which, to be effective, must remain one.

* * *

Torah, translated *nomos* (law) by the Septuagint, means the *teaching*. *Torah* comes from *yrh*, to teach, show, instruct, distinguish. The translation of *torah* by "law" merely contributes to strengthen the fallacy that represents the biblical contribution as an ethics.

The *torah* is not a system of interdictions, not a moral code. It is rather a pedagogy of understanding and of liberty. Understanding and liberty are interdependent since knowledge and action are inseparable. The precept that commands an action arouses the mind at the same time: "Through your commandments you have made me wiser than my enemies.... I have more understanding than all my teachers for your testimonies are my meditation... I understand more than the ancients.... Through your precepts I get understanding... The entrance of your words gives understanding to the simple...." [1]

The Mosaic law is contemplation: "Open my eyes that I may see the wonders of your Torah... Give me understanding that I may keep your Torah and that I may observe it with my whole heart... I will delight myself in your Torah... O how I love your Torah, it is my meditation all the day..." [2]

---

[1] Ps. 119.   [2] Ps. 119.

"Hearken unto me, my people... for the Torah shall proceed from me, and I shall establish my commandment to be a light for the peoples." [1] "The commandment is a light." *

"I have taught you statutes and judgments as Yhwh my God commanded me, that you should practice them in the land where you go to possess it.   Observe them and put them to practice, for this is your wisdom *(hokemah,* LXX: *sophia),* and your understanding *(binah, sunesis)* in the sight of the nations, which shall hear all these statutes and say: Surely this nation is a wise and understanding people" *(hokam wenabōn, sophos kai epistēmōn).* [2]

---

[1] Is. 51: 4.
* Prov. 6: 23, and it is prophetic: "The law having a shadow of things to come" Heb. 10: 1.
[2] Deut. 4: 5, 6.

chapter three

SPIRITUAL UNDERSTANDING : FAITH

Understanding is a discernment of that which is principle and germ in a growing world and in history.

All creation starts from a germ. All creation is a germination. The germ is in the beginning. The germ is the principle. But it is also the end, for the organism's fulfilment is a revelation of what was implied in the seed. Indeed, organism and germ are not two distinct things. The organism is but the germ in its plenitude, one might say: the germ, totally expressed. *

What Bergson said of the intellectual seed from which a work grows can very well be applied to the biological germ: it is the work's "dynamic pattern," an "inner principle of direction," ** a "waiting for images."

Sensible reality is being elaborated. Now what works upon it is, itself, neither sensible nor visible. *Natura naturata* is indeed

---

* "Between impulse and attraction, between the 'efficient cause' and the 'final cause' there is, we believe, an intermediary something, a form of activity from which the philosophers have drawn by impoverishment and dissociation (and by moving out to the two extreme and opposite limits), the idea of efficient cause on the one hand and that of final cause on the other. This operation, which is that of life itself, is a gradual transition from the less fulfilled to the more fulfilled, from intensive to extensive, from a mutual implication of the parts to their juxtaposition" (BERGSON, *L'Energie Spirituelle*, p. 190, P.U.F. 1946).

** According to Bergson evolution reveals such a principle of direction. "It looks as if some imprecise and diffuse being, that we may call, as we please, man or super-man, had sought to realize himself and had succeeded only by foresaking a part of himself on the way". (*L'Evolution créatrice*, p. 267, P.U.F. 1946). "Thus, in final analysis man would be the motive for the organization of all of life on this planet." (*L'Evolution créatrice*, p.186; cf. *Les Deux Sources de la Morale et de la Religion*, p. 271, P.U.F. 1946).

The idea of a man or a super-man being the germ of evolution calls to mind the doctrine of Adam-Kadmon in the Cabala and, going further back, the messianism of the prophets. "The end would be reached only if there finally appeared what should theoretically have existed from the beginning: a divine humanity."

visible, but *natura naturans*, by its very essence, is not. The sensible is never but a moment, but a passage. Not a principle, not an end, by its nature it is ephemeral. And so, while we see these accidentals, the essential is hidden, through a metaphysical necessity: *deus absconditus*.

If we wish to have a realistic and faithful conception of some living reality, a plant for instance, then we must not rest with what we see. Instead we, who live as the plant lives, must orient our minds to its maturation, follow in mind the dynamics of the plant's creation and move with it to the as yet invisible fruit. If we stop at the visible, if we stumble upon it and cling to the present flower, we are distracted from the real, perceiving a merely transitory aspect of the living plant. For the flower we see is already of the past and the fruit yet invisible is already more real. Only through such a tension does the plant live, only through this drive to fruition. A faithful conception of the living plant will, with the plant, hope for the fruit to come, which is the plant's justification. Any attachment to the flower in its beauty is an inversion. For a true understanding of reality is hopefulness. There is a dynamics in understanding that relates it to the genesis, the progressive creation of reality. And any thought is unreal that does not take into account this immanent act of creation: "for the figure of this world shall pass." [1]

By their essence, sensible things are perishable. "We look, not to the visible things, but to the invisible; for the visible things are but for a time, whereas the invisible are eternal." [2]

The Bible's conception of understanding is related to its conception of time, a genesis of reality. Hope is that virtue of the spirit that links the spirit to this creation perpetually at work.

Thus failure, in Hebrew thought with its conception of time-creation, cannot have the same significance as it would in a completed cosmos where time has no function. In a world that is definite and complete, failure is viewed as a thing against which one comes to a halt. But in a world that is being invented, failure is never something static. It is only a moment, a phase in a process of creation, of parturition. "In sorrow shalt thou bring forth children." "A woman when she is in labor has sorrow because her hour is come." [3] Within an evolution failure has a sense. "For we know that all creation groans and travails in pain together until now." [4]

---

[1] I Cor. 7: 31.
[3] John 16: 12.
[2] 2 Cor. 4: 18.
[4] Rom. 8: 22.

In a fixed and settled universe — in Cartesian time which is a trickle of unrelated instants, or in Kantian time which is a receptacle — hope suffers from the dichotomy of Zeno of Eleas. It is noteworthy that the despair and the sentiment of absurdity in the modern philosophies are bound to a Cartesian or Kantian conception of time.

* * *

That spiritual, supernatural, understanding which is faith is an awareness of the Germ at work within creation, creation's principle and reason. "Now faith is the substance of things hoped for, the evidence of things not seen.... By faith we do recognize that the world was formed by the word of God in such a way that the things that we see were not made from visible things." [1]

In the Old Testament the prophets often refer to the Anointed as the Germ, *tsemach*. * "My servant the Germ." [2] "Behold a man whose name is Germ, he shall germinate out of his place, and he shall build the temple of Yhwh." [3] "I shall raise unto David a righteous germ." [4] "In that day shall the germ of Yhwh be beautiful and glorious." [5] "There will I make the horn of David to bud (to germinate), I have ordained a lamp for mine anointed." [6]

The germ by which the world was made, and by which creation now continues, is not only biological. It is a spiritual Germ. God is Pneuma. The Germ is Logos. "In the beginning was the Logos, all things were made by him, and without him nothing was made that was made." [7] The Logos is not only a Germ of life, but also of light: "...in him was life, and the life was the light of men." [8]

Now this Germ is Word, which means that it is essentially significant. When he comes in the flesh, each gesture, each act of the incarnate Logos will be a sign, *sēmeion*. Faith reads a meaning, discerns the Word beneath the sensible aspect of these signs. Understanding is an ability to read these signs. The biblical conception of understanding is linked to its conception of the

---

[1] Heb. 11: 1, 3.
* The customary English rendering of *Tsemach* is *Branch*.   Germ is however the more precise translation.   (*Translator's note*)
[2] Zach. 3: 8.   [3] Zach. 6: 12.
[4] Jer. 23: 5.   [5] Is. 4: 2.
[6] Ps. 132: 17.   [7] John 1.
[8] *Ibid.*

sensible's significance, and of reality's continuous creation, the Germ of which reality is a Word.

The meaning itself is not sensible but must be discerned within the sensible. It is the very essence of understanding not to stop at the visible sign, but to move on, through it, to the meaning. "Because that which may be known of God is manifest in them. For God has shown it unto them. For the things invisible to Him, from the creation of the world are clearly seen, being understood by the things that are made; His eternal power also, and His divinity...." [1]

To read a meaning in something perceived is an action; it does not take place apart from the dynamism of the subject. No apperception is passive. It is always a dialogue between what is perceived and the person who perceives, a flow from one to the other, an exchange. The weak and the sick who can no longer bring their own contribution to this exchange will no longer perceive the meaning immanent to reality. Thenceforth the world will seem a meaningless kaleidoscope: "For unto everyone that has shall be given, and he shall have abundance, but from him that has not shall be taken away even that which he has." [2] "For those who are outside, everything is a parable... that listening they may hear and not understand." [3]

Faith is a reading of a certain datum in which the act of understanding proceeds from the Spirit's inhabitation. Faith, we repeat is, *sunesis pneumatikē*, [4] a spiritual understanding.

* * *

Faith *is* understanding.

Nothing is more counter to the biblical theology of faith, and its conception of understanding, than the Cartesian dichotomies between "natural reason" and "faith." *   Faith is not fideism.

---

[1] Rom. 1: 19-20.   [2] Matth. 25: 29.
[3] Mark 4: 11.   [4] Col. 1: 9.
* "Now the sovereign good considered by natural reason and without the light of faith..." (*Principes*, pref. A.T., IX, 4). According to Descartes "faith" is the object of will, not of mind: "...quae divinitus revelata sunt, omni cognitione certiora credamus, cum illorum fides, quaecumque est de obscuris, non ingenii actio est, sed voluntaris." (*Reg.* III, A.T., X, p. 270). "The great difference between acquired truth and revealed truth is that the knowledge of the latter depends only upon grace (which God denies to no-one though it be not effective in all); the most idiotic and the most simple can therefore succeed in this just

Faith, *pistis*, in the New Testament, is what the prophets called understanding and knowledge. The *pistis* of the New Testament has too often been confused with the *pistis* of Plato which is one of the last and lowest modes of knowledge, even unworthy of the name of knowledge. [1] In other words the *pistis* of the New Testament has been confused with *belief*. Thus faith becomes an unintelligible monster. Fideism is a latent heresy, an infantile disease that has ruled many minds since Descartes and Pascal.

In the New Testament, faith is understanding and knowledge. "Have you understood all these things?" [2] "Listen and understand." [3] "Are you also still without understanding?" [4] "Do you not yet understand?" [5] "Are you so without understanding also?" [6] "Do you not yet perceive nor understand?" [7] "How is it that you do not understand?" [8] "Let the reader understand." [9]

In the Gospel of John the link between faith and understanding is clear in many texts. "We *believe* and we *know* that you are the Holy One of God." [10] "They have *known* surely that I came out from You, and they have *believed* that it is You Who sent me." [11] "And we have *known* and *believed*." [12] Witness also the juncture of the two texts: "...if you do not *believe* that I am..." (John 8: 24), and "...Then you will know that I am..." (8: 28). (Cf. Jer. 24: 7: "I shall give them a heart to know me.")

The first commandment is "to love God... with all one's understanding." [13] Faith in the words of St. Paul, is "an understanding of the mystery of Christ." * "We do not cease praying

---

as well as the most subtle" (Letter to — 1638). "... I do not here take into account divine revelation because it does not lead us by degrees but lifts us all at once to an infallible belief" (Principes, lettre de l'auteur). Faith to Descartes is really a belief and not knowledge nor intelligence. "The revealed truths are above our intelligence..." (*Discours*, 1st part). On this point cf. BLONDEL, *Le Christianisme de Descartes*, in *Revue de Métaphysique et de Morale*, 1896, and also the essays of Laberthonnière.

[1] *Republic*, Book 6.
[3] Matth. 15: 10.
[5] Matth. 16: 9.
[7] Mark 8: 17.
[9] Mark 13: 14.
[11] John 17: 8.
[13] Mark 12: 33.

[2] Matth. 13: 51.
[4] Matth. 15: 16.
[6] Mark 7: 8.
[8] Mark 8: 21.
[10] John 6: 69.
[12] 1 John 4: 16.

* *Mystery* today means something impenetrable to the mind, something never to be understood. To St. Paul and to the early Christian thinkers it was on the contrary the particular objet of intelligence, its fullest nourishment. The *musterion* is something so rich in intelligible content, so inexhaustibly full of delectation for the mind that no contemplation can ever reach its end. It is an eternal delectation for the mind.

for you, asking that you be filled with the knowledge of (God's) will, in all wisdom and spiritual understanding." [1]

Faith is an assent to truth, *pistis alētheias.* ★ Because it is an understanding it requires attentiveness: *pistis ex akoēs,* [2] "faith by hearing." And because it is a spiritual, supernatural understanding, it is also a "mystery": "Holding the mystery of faith in a pure mind." [3]

That spiritual (supernatural) understanding which is faith, is rooted in the secret recesses of the heart, at the very base of our being. It defines this being's essence, whose main action it is. It is a sign of the fundamental choice, the answer that cannot be constrained. Jesus asks: "Do you believe this?" [4] "Do you believe that I can do this? And they said: Yes, Lord. Then he touched their eyes saying: Let it be done to you according to your faith." [5] The answer that Jesus awaits with an infinite respect reveals an inner dialogue hidden in the heart of man, between the Holy Spirit and the spirit of man, a dialogue of two liberties. "Blessed are you, Simon Peter..." [6] "Hearing this Jesus was in admiration, and said to those that were with Him: ...in no person in Israel have I found so great a faith." [7] "Great is your faith." [8] This is the only compliment that Jesus ever pays. For faith is a value, the prime value, as understanding and knowledge were in the Old Testament. *Pistis* is a continuation of what the Old Testament calls knowledge of Yhwh, understanding.

Pistis is man's essential act, the one act which defines him. "Whoever believes in Him is not condemned, but whoever does not believe is already condemned because he has not believed in the name of God's only Son. And this is the condemnation: it is that the Light came into the world, and that men preferred darkness to light because their works were evil." [9]

As did the prophets before Him, Jesus reproaches His hearers with their lack of understanding: "O men without understanding and slow of heart to believe all that the prophets have said." [10]

---

[1] Col. 1: 9.
★ 2 Thes. 2: 13. *Pistis alētheias* is the complete Hebrew translation of *hēmouna*: *hēmouna* is derived from *hemet* which means truth.
[2] Rom. 10: 17.   [3] 1 Tim. 3: 9.
[4] John 11: 26.   [5] Matth. 9: 28.
[6] Matth. 16: 17.
[7] Matth. 8: 10; cf. Luke 7: 9; Matth. 9: 2, etc.
[8] Matth. 15: 28.   [9] John 3: 18.
[10] Luke 24: 25.

Everywhere the heart's own freedom is important in the act of understanding: "the heart believes to its own justification." [1]

Whe have seen that in the Old Testament understanding and knowledge are the foremost virtues: Yhwh prefers knowledge of Him to sacrifices.

In the New Testament we find the same idea transposed: faith, *pistis* is justice, is justification. It is that because it is an expression of the essential act that defines a man, proceeding from his "heart." That justice of action and thought (the *zedaka*), which is "to know Yhwh," finds its supreme criterion in faith. Faith, *pistis*, reveals the prime choice secretly made, the choice that is part of man's very substance. It is so much a part of it in fact, that he may never separate himself from the Yes or the No spoken in the depths of his heart.

This is the idea developed by St. Paul when he says that "man is justified by faith." [2]

The understanding which is faith, reveals the heart's lack of duplicity, what the New Testament calls purity: "...having purified their hearts by faith." [3]

As we saw with understanding in the Old Testament, *pistis* is the relationship of two liberties, the liberty of God, the giver, and the liberty of man. This is why Paul calls faith "the justice (the righteousness) of God," "the justice of God by faith." [4]

---

[1] Rom. 10: 10.
[2] Rom. 3: 28; cf. 3: 22; 3: 26; Gal. 2: 16, etc.
[3] Acts 15: 9.   [4] Rom. 3: 22.

chapter four

THE " RENEWAL OF THE INTELLECT "
AND CHRISTIAN PHILOSOPHY

Faith is not opposed to reason. The conflict is one between two definitions of reason. The Bible's teaching is not opposed to Greek philosophy as a "faith" to rational thought. It is rather the opposition of one system of thought to another one of radically different structure.

From the very start the Greek categories and the Hebrew forms of thought are heterogenous. The problems are differently put. So we cannot pass from the universe of Greek thought to the biblical world unless we forsake the Greek perspectives — "go out from the midst of her, my people" — and unless we wholly transform the system of references and of coordinates. This transformation is effected by opening up a new dimension: the spiritual.

The analysis of the specific forms and the original problematic of Hebrew thought necessarily obliges us to question the categories and the problematic of Greek philosophy. Indeed, unless we do question the implicit *a priori* and the unconscious intellectual habits of Western philosophy — habits all the more tyrannical because they are unconscious — we shall be unable to discover and understand the characteristics and the structure of Hebrew thought. By reflection on this Hebrew problematic from which we have become estranged, the "unseen essential" which governs our own minds will come to light.

The developments of modern science, the discovery of non-Euclidean geometries, of non-Newtonian mechanics, have challenged all the logical *a priori* of Euclid's geometry and of Newton's physics which, to Kant, seemed the necessary expression of the forms of our understanding. "We must learn a lesson from this... Reason must submit to science. Geometry, physics and arithmetic are sciences, whereas the traditional doctrine of an absolute and immutable reason is but a philosophy. It is an obsolete philosophy." [1]

The metaphysics of the sensible implied in the biblical narratives goes quite against Greek thought's most fundamental attitudes in regard to reality, time, the multiple and the becoming. Biblical metaphysics and Neo-Platonism flow in opposite directions. As we have seen, the deep-rooted dualism in Greek thought makes the major themes of biblical thought seem intolerable paradoxes. The Greek intelligence cannot accept the ideas that give biblical tradition its specific orientation. These ideas go against the grain of Greek habits of thought, against the innermost movement of Greek ideas.

The ideas of creation, incarnation, inhabitation of the Spirit, presence of the supernatural are all interdependent. The Incarnation is the real presence of God to His created work: His presence in His written word, the inspired Books, the presence of the Logos come in the flesh, His presence in the Body which is the Church and in the substantial words which are the sacraments.

All these themes move against a slope made very steep by old, habits of thought that are more or less conscious. One would have to analyze all the prejudices that make the idea of creation unacceptable to a Greek mind, even though creation itself is one of the facts most constantly manifest all around us. There is a certain conception of the sensible that makes the idea of incarnation unacceptable, and the real presence remains a paradox to any dualistic and more or less Manichean metaphysics.

The usual temptation for a Greek mind whose *a priori* are strongly crystallized is to reject unequivocally the material that it cannot assimilate — thus with Plotinus or Spinoza — or at least to try to reduce the new world of thought to its own dimensions, to the dimensions of the old world. This reduction is accomplished by casting out the original dimensions that are specifically the Bible's: creation, the incarnation, and "spirit" in the biblical sense *(pneuma)*, that is the supernatural.

This has been the work of the Gnostics. The Gnostic effort has been permanent, has been constantly repeated, from the day of the

---

[1] G. BACHELARD, *La philosophie du non*, in fine.

first Christian Gnostics, up to Leibnitz and Hegel. In these it finds a particularly magnificent expression, nurtured by the Cabala's esoterism and by the great philosophic wealth of Neo-Platonism. Alongside Christian philosophy and theology, the Gnostic intuitions have built up a sort of *"philosophia perennis"* which, to certain minds, is all the more fascinating because they come upon it as their own invention, as a conception familiar to them. To a certain number of people there naturally exists a Gnostic church, because there is a Gnostic *spirit* that leads spontaneously to certain metaphysical solutions.

There are two aspects to the Gnostic illusion.

(1) The first is the belief arising out of a series of assumptions on the nature of the sensible, the concrete, the existent, which are the assumptions of Platonism and of Manichean dualism — that there is *more* to be found in an allegorical interpretation of the Bible than in its literal truth, *more* in a Docetist view of creation and incarnation than in their historical reality, *more* in the abstract symbol than in the concrete fact. This attempt to do away with the historical and the carnal was made in the name of an interpretation "in spirit and in truth." The Gnostics confused the abstract, the disincarnate and the spiritual. But, as we have seen, the disincarnate is not in itself spiritual. This confusion leads us to the second aspect of the Gnostic illusion.

(2) The second aspect is an unawareness of the significance of the *pneuma*, the spirit, in biblical tradition. To a Docetism evacuating the creation and the incarnation there corresponds a theory of salvation that evacuates the supernatural.

Therefore in this second respect, the Gnostic illusion is to have assumed, in complete ignorance of supernatural essence of faith and charity, which belong to the order of pneuma, that there is *more* to be found in the noetic "Gnostic" *interpretation* than in the spiritual theological *virtues* of faith and charity. The Gnostic fails to see that *there is, on the contrary, more, and not less, in faith and charity, even from the point of view of knowledge,* than there is in the Gnostic philosophic systems which depend on *"nous"* instead of *"pneuma."*

The great Gnostic intuitions are truly admirable. They have seduced men of such genius as Leibnitz and Hegel. Nevertheless they manifest an incurable blindness with respect to the supernatural dimension of the biblical revelation, and a radical misunderstanding of Christianity's specific nature.

* * *

The transition from the perspectives of Greek philosophy to those of the biblical world can only be made through a total renewal of the mind, what St. Paul calls the "renewal of the intellect": "Do not conform to this world but be transformed by the renewal of the intellect." [1]   This renewal of the mind is effected by the Spirit: *"be renewed by the spirit of your mind."*   (*anaeneoustai tō pneumati tou noos humōn*). *

Christian philosophy grows from this renewal of the intelligence.

Of course, if, by "philosophy," we mean Greek philosophy exclusively, then there is definitely no Christian philosophy. And if by "reason" we mean the categories of Greek thought, then certainly the content of the Bible is not "rational."   But does this have any meaning beyond this single quite contingent fact: that the profound structure of Greek thought is not the same as that of biblical thought?   From this disparity are we authorized to deduce any legitimate condemnation?   Indeed the whole question is to decide whether the forms of Greek reason are those of human reason.   It should be noted that these categories reveal themselves every day less capable of grasping reality such as physics, biology and psychology now unfold it.   In science too, we must renew the categories of our intelligence.   In this state of affairs, it seems a good omen for biblical thought that its own place is on the side of living reality.   Can Greek logic understand the growth of a tree out of its seed?

It is a property of Christian philosophy that it does not try to reject the terms of biblical thought simply because they are hard to assimilate for a form of intelligence, which in the words of Bergson, is characterized by a "natural incomprehension of life."

In the minds of the Prophets and the Apostles no opposition exists between faith and understanding.   *Stupidity* and *folly* are the contrary of the spiritual understanding of faith, a stupidity and a folly which are a hardening, an aberration of the heart, the result of a secret choice made in the darkness of man's primordial freedom.   The opposition of faith and reason is an idea of the

---

[1] Rom. 12: 2.

* Ephes. 4: 23. *Metanoia* which is translated conversion or repentance really means something quite different.   It is truly a "renewal of the intellect" which makes understanding possible, a renewal of what the Old Testament called the "heart," the place of the essential choice by which we act and know.   The first word of Jesus in the Gospel of Mark (the Gospel closest to the source) is: *Metanoiete kai pisteuete en tō euangeliō,* "renew your hearts, your minds and believe in the good news" (Mark 1: 15).

philosophers, those philosophers who "realized" the structure and categories of Greek thought without understanding the import of the renewal of the intellect through the spirit which is the fruit of the Gospel and of baptism.

The Christian is a "new creature," a "new man." The wisdom of Christianity holds nothing in common with the wisdom of the Greek philosophers. The Christian does not seek "happiness" *(eudaimōnia)* ; he does not believe himself justified by "virtue" *(arētē)* ; nor is his ultimate aim the "supreme good." The different forms of pagan wisdom have always been more or less of an *accommodation*, the art of resigning oneself to man's condition. But Christianity is not an ethics.

From the Greek point of view the wisdom proposed by Christianity is a *hubris*, a monstrously scandalous demand; for the Christian asks for nothing less than participation in the life of God. He asks to become a god himself and to be adopted as a son by the Holy Trinity. The Christian's hope is "folly" or idiocy in the sight of a Plotinus or a Spinoza.

"However we proclaim wisdom among the perfect: yet not the wisdom of this world nor of the princes of this world that come to naught. But we proclaim the wisdom of God in a mystery, a hidden wisdom, which God ordained before the world unto our glory: which none of the princes of this world knew." [1] The only thing in common between Christian wisdom and the wisdom of the philosophers is the name. By its content Christian wisdom belongs to another order, the supernatural. The categories of ancient wisdom — happiness, virtue, good — cannot be transposed into this new dimension. All is different here, even language.

"Beware lest any man cheat you by philosophy and vain deceit according to the tradition of men, according to the rudiments of the world, and not according to Christ: for in Him dwells all the fulness of the Godhead bodily." [2]

* * *

It is through their sense of contemplation that Plato, Aristotle and Plotinus have something in common with the Prophets of Israel. At the height of Greek philosophy it is this love of contemplation found in the *Symposium*, the *Phaedros*, the tenth

[1] I Cor. 2: 6, 8.   [2] Col. 2: 8, 9.

book of the *Nichomachean Ethics*, book Λ of the *Metaphysics* and in those treatises of the Enneads that speak of love and beauty, that prepares the encounter with the biblical message.

Nevertheless, contemplation does not have the same metaphysical structure in both traditions.

The Greek idea of contemplation is founded on the dualism between matter and the Idea, between action and the theoretical life, between contingent existence and necessary essence. Contemplation therefore is linked to *leisure*. It cannot be reconciled with work. It is, according to Plato and Plotinus, an evasion, *fugē*.

In the biblical tradition, on the contrary, contemplation does not exclude work. The contrary of contemplation is not action but *care*. *

Contemplation of the biblical sort is nourished by the sensible realities of everyday life. It is incarnated. Platonic contemplation is disincarnated.

In biblical thought contemplation uses the mediation of concrete, carnal reality. It is realized in action. The highest contemplation is at once the most efficient action. Contemplation operates *within* work and action. When the Word was made flesh, he chose this sort of life, a life of work and action. And yet this life in no way impeded his incessant contemplation of the Father. Instead it made it manifest.

It is very important for Christians to distinguish Platonic contemplation and the contemplation of the Gospels. The first is a natural effort of the soul to leave the body and the world. The latter is a dialogue with God that transforms the world. It is supernatural and incarnated.

* ** *

There are certain metaphysical exigences implied in revelation, and organically prerequisite to revelation. There is a metaphysical substructure pre-adapted to the theological message delivered by the inspired books. This revealed theological message could not have been expressed in just any metaphysics, or incarnated in just any kind of thought structure. Platonism, for instance, by

---

* Cf. Appendix II.

its very nature was incapable of receiving or sustaining the biblical theology of creation, the incarnation and the real presence.

These metaphysical requirements prerequisite to the epiphany of the revealed message remain the metaphysical requirements of a theology which proceeds from the biblical revelation, which prolongs it by making it explicit (as the seed, in its growth, manifests what it contains), and which faithfully safeguards the revealed deposit in the process of thinking it out.   In Blondel's phrase, these are "the philosophical exigences of Christianity."

There is a Christian philosophy because there is a pagan problematic incompatible with the biblical revelation.

To deny that there are metaphysical exigences vitally prerequired to revelation, and to the theology that proceeds from revelation, is to assume that revelation could have been made anywhere, at any time, and without a long preparation of man.   And this would amount to saying that revelation merely superimposed itself on some given human mentality in an entirely external manner.   To say this is to forget that revelation is an incarnation.

Because there is a cooperation between God's freedom and the freedom of man, the incarnation is a dialogue between God and man, a dialogue in which man readies himself for the Coming, and if one may so speak, goes a little way toward the encounter with Him who comes.

The Incarnation would never have been possible without that *fiat* slowly brought to maturity by a whole people, throughout the course of its long history, to emerge in utterance upon the lips of a virgin of Israel.

Revelation is the incarnation of a theology in a human thought structure and a human language, therefore — before any revelation could be made — this thought structure — Hebrew thought — had to be predisposed to receive the word of the living God, just as, later, a virgin of Israel was predisposed to receive and to bear the Word, who was made flesh that He might manifest Himself to us.

---

* Cf. Appendix III, *Hebrew Thought and the Church.*

Conclusion

Let us imagine an industrialist who wants his son to become an executive like himself. He, the father, has struggled, suffered, and created his work, this great industry, with his intelligence and his genius. He wants his son to be in every way like him: a creator. He wants him to know the godlike joys of creation, and wants him to be worthy of the fortune and honor that will be his.

What will he do, then? Will he just leave the industry to his son, once he is grown up?

Surely he will not. For if he did, his son would not become a creator like himself, a man in his own image, but a passive and unworthy heir, a being that is capable only of receiving, but incapable of giving or creating.

The father loves his son too much to consent to this. If he gave him the fruit of his genius and of his own work without requiring anything, he would deprive him of the best of life: the joy of liberty and of creation. The father wants his son to be like him, a man whom he can treat as an equal, a friend worthy of him.

So what the son must do is in some way recreate, through his own work, the industry that his father built and that will some day be his. Such are the requirements of the father's love.

Now God was faced, I might say, with a metaphysical problem analogous to this. He neither wanted to create a mere living puppet that would be His tool, nor a happy and obedient animal, but a being in His own "image and likeness," [1] that is, according to the Scriptures, a god: "I said: you are gods." [2] Christ quotes this in answer to the Jews: "it is not written in your law: I said: you are gods." [3]

God has no use for submissive slaves. It was His wish to create beings that could actually partake of His trinitary life, and of the joys of the three Creator-persons of the Holy Unity. Otherwise

---

[1] Gen. 1: 26.   [2] Ps. 82: 6.

[3] John 10: 34.

how could Wisdom say: "My delights are to be with the children of men." [1]

What seems to have been the method, the stratagem God used to solve this, the most fundamental of all metaphysical problems: *How was He to create beings like Himself, the uncreated Creator, who, although they have nothing they have not received, and would be nothing had He not created them, would be worthy of partaking of His life and of His joy?*

Here we have the primordial metaphysical problem: the problem of coexistence of the many and the One, of beings and of Being, of the free action of persons in the presence of the free Action of God. It is "that problem so long argued by the old philosophers: how could a multiplicity of any sort, a dyad or a number, come into being out of the One as we have defined him? How is it that the One did not remain within himself?" [2] As we have seen, Plotinus, along with all Neo-Platonic metaphysics, explains this existence of the multiple by a degradation and a fall from the One. The problem of action and of freedom is solved in the same way: individual action is reabsorbed into cosmic action by conversion, consent, and resignation. *

Biblical metaphysics gives another answer: the *reason* for the creation of the multitude of beings, the *reason* for the existence of free and creative persons is *love*.

This love requires autonomous *persons* to answer it.

Now what was, according to the Scriptures, the method used by God to satisfy the requirement of this love?

At the term of the long labor of creation of matter and life, at the end of time (in the final flowering of biological evolution, we might say now in the language of science), God calls forth a being that is, in its biological structure, an animal, and yet that bears within itself — "we have this treasure in earthen vessels" — a call, the earnest of a supernatural destiny. This *desiderium naturale*, is the consubstantial desire ** to rise to participation in the Creator's life: *assimilari Deo*. The immanence of the *pneuma*, its inhabitation in man, is the pledge and the promise of a transformation that will make man a "joint-heir with Christ."

But, in the accomplishment of this transformation, man must *co-operate*. Here we discover what we have presumed to call

---

[1] Prov. 8: 31.   [2] PLOTINUS, *Enn.* 5: 1, 6.
* Cf. The Stoics and Spinoza.
** A desire that is a part of the substance of man.

God's stratagem: this latest creature, of whom God said: "let us make man in our image, after our likeness," this last come among the inhabitants of the earth, is as yet *incomplete*. Man has not yet reached the plenitude he is destined to reach.

This is, we feel, the dialectic moment signified in the Bible by the episode of the Garden of Eden and of the temptation.

* [*] *

The idea of a progressive *plan* in the creation of man, the idea of a maturation, the idea of some sort of necessary development and transformation foreseen even in the primitive economy and intended to lead man to his adult state, the state of a son of God, seems to be implied by the entire biblical conception of time and history, by God's injunctions in the first chapter of Genesis: "Be fruitful, and multiply and replenish the earth," and by certain texts of the Apostle Paul. [1]

God's method, the only method His love would allow, is to create a being that might create himself in order truly to become a god, a being in the image and after the likeness of the Creator.

To object that man cannot create himself, since he was necessarily created by God, is to ignore God's gift and to assume that God creates alone. But it was God's wish to create a god, a creator. There can very well be symbiosis of God's creative action and the creative action of man, whom He created. We *are* co-creators with God: "*Theou gar esmen sunergoi.*" [2]

"My destiny holds nothing arbitrary nor tyrannical for the slightest pressure from the outside would suffice to deprive being of all value, of all beauty, of all consistency. I have nothing that I have not received, and yet everything, at the same time, must arise from me, even the being that I have received and that seems imposed on me. Whatever I do and whatever I undergo I must sanction this being and so to speak engender it anew by my personal consent without ever letting my most sincere freedom disavow it." [3]

God's creative action chose this paradox: to raise other creative actions in its own image and likeness.

* [*] *

---

[1] Cf. Part II, Chap. 2.
[2] I Cor. 3: 9; cf. Part I, Chap. 3.   [3] M. BLONDEL, *L'Action*, pp. XXIII, XXIV.

"Original sin" is a "specific" sin. It is the sin of a species: man. *Ha-Adam* means man, humanity. It is a collective noun at least in a number of texts. Adam's sin is "original" chronologically, but even more so ontologically. When the Bible speaks of "the sin of Judah," or the iniquity of "Ephraim," these proper names are being used patronymically. The Bible also speaks of "the sin of Sodom," or the "sin of Jerusalem" in a collective sense.

Animals live with the assurance, elegance, and silent wisdom immanent to life and to instinct. Risk appears with man, with consciousness; for man knows what is good and bad for him.

Genesis tells us that this knowledge of what is good and what is bad was promptly followed by a loss of assurance and a feeling of fear, of fear before God. Discovering that he is naked, man hides himself. Until then, he was naked but he "felt no shame." Now "he knows that he is naked," "his eyes have been opened." He discovers his ontological nakedness, his essential deficiency. So he clothes himself, (his clothing is a concealment of himself from his own eyes) and hides from his Creator. We encounter this same fear all through the Bible. Henceforth the vision of God is felt as a mortal danger to man. "You cannot see my face: for no man shall see Me and live." [1] "Let not God speak to us, lest we die." [2] "We shall certainly die because we have seen God." [3] "Woe is me for I am undone, for I am a man of unclean lips... and mine eyes have seen the King, the Lord of Hosts." [4]

In Genesis God asks this surprising question: "Who told you that you were naked?" Previously man was naked but he did not feel that his nakedness was a privation; he did not know what he lacked.

* * *

Man must "create" himself. He must give his consent and work with God his transformation, a transformation that will allow him to participate in his Creator's life. With the appearance of man the act of creation, which we may follow as it unfolds in the course of time into branches of ever more complex species, ceases to be the sole conscious act. It has now brought conscience into the very beings it engenders. And along with conscience come risk and the possibility of failure. But this very possibility is implied in the requirements of God's love.

---

[1] Ex. 33: 20. [2] Ex. 20: 19.
[3] Jud. 13: 22. [4] Is. 6: 5.

God is more demanding than we ourselves are, regarding our beatitude. It is a god's joy that he prepares for us. To envision God's design upon us we must exhaust our imagination and know that we will still be underestimating its goodness. For the best and the most beautiful that any speculation can construct is still a shadow of what God holds in store for us. Our hopes will always be avaricious. Heresies have been this impotence to dare hope for the most. The Bible's metaphysics is a metaphysics of *Yes*: "For the Son of God, Jesus Christ, was not *Yes* and *No*, but Yes was in Him. For all the promises of God in Him are Yes, and in Him Amen." [1] He is the "Amen," [2] the total Yes. God's own measure is superabundance. Some of us may believe that they would have been content with an eternal human happiness. But it is God's will that we become gods in His image. The danger of failure is implied in this supreme vocation. By the very fact that there is a growth and maturation in which we must co-operate, the danger also exists that we may go against growth, refuse and invert the plan of God. God cannot force us: a god is not constrained. He calls us. He pleads with us. He presses us. But He would not violate this freedom, the very essence of His creation.

Throughout the Old Testament God's pedagogical method with Israel, His child, is not a method of constraint. He could very well have forced obedience to His will. But He preferred to draw, *from man's own freedom*, an answer, a love, a return to God. It is really a wonder of God's work that He provoked this "stiff-necked people" to produce such admirable answers, the founts of holiness from Abraham to the prophets, without constraint, without destroying the freedom out of which these answers must spring. Yhwh never uses Israel like a tool. He solicits, He pleads: "Listen, Israel..."

History reveals God's method to us. Suffering is an element of it. But suffering in itself does not purify. It has too often and unthinkingly been said that it does. No, suffering and failure are an intervention of God meant to prevent man from *settling* in a condition that is not his vocation, which is beatitude.

In the history of Israel, as later in the history of the Church, enemies and adversaries have a providential function. Each time the Church loses or neglects a part of truth entrusted to her, an adversary is raised to attack her, in the defense of this partial truth:

---

[1] 2 Cor. 1: 18.   [2] Apoc. 3: 14.

Thus the Renaissance which saved the Church from the temptations of temporal government and intellectual tyranny; thus Nietzsche who helps us not to reduce Christianity to the level of a morbid ethics; thus Freud, and Marx. Each adversary in his time was made necessary by a failing of Christendom. Thus, if Christendom no longer goes to the poor, others will go to them, proclaiming justice. And at the same time they will attack the Church, batter the Church, as once the Assyrian and the Egyptian attacked and destroyed Israel when she was unfaithful to her God and to the covenant. Truth no longer admits being absent from the world. When Truth is not served with sufficient energy by the Body charged with its keeping, it will look elsewhere for men to serve the portions neglected by Christendom. But this servant will rise up to war against Jerusalem. It is as if Truth could not stand division; the face of war is the face of Truth divided. War *means* that Truth wants to be reunited. * When Israel is overrun by the Assyrian, a prophet appears and explains their failure and suffering to the people and calls them back to Yhwh. God gives His people no peace when they turn from the destiny which is their life. "I have loved thee with an everlasting love, O virgin of Israel." [1]

* * *

History is the growth of mankind, moving to its adult state; a growth very different from the gentle growth of plants. We discover a *negative* element in the history of man. "In sorrow shalt thou bring forth children."

This negative quantity appears ever more clearly as humanity grows. By analogy with individual life and psychoanalysis, we might say that sin is abreacted in history. By observing his own

---

* What is the significance of war (in the sense in which we might inquire into the significance of a neurosis)? In the individual: illness, conscious or unconscious conflict, contain both a negative and a positive aspect. Fever is a battle to return to health: better this inner war than the pacification of death.

Between persons, reproach, complaint, imply a demand for perfection, a healthy dissatisfaction.

Lovers are dissatisfied with one another because neither is God for the other. Reproach, complaint can be fruitful. If I am too weak or too self-satisfied to judge myself, then others will do it.

Between nations, the conflict within mankind, within the total Adam, shows an inability to be satisfied with a state of things which, in fact, is not the term of human destiny.

[1] Jer. 31: 3.

actions Adam becomes aware of what was hidden in his heart from the very beginning. Thus he is delivered of it. We only know the tree by its fruits. "There is nothing hidden that shall not be uncovered, and nothing secret that shall not be known." [1] Thus the term of the growth will be the time of full awareness. Thereby "we know that it is the last time." [2] According to the prophets the history of man must end with unremitting war.

* * *

This is our vocation, this is our foremost duty: we must create. "Be fruitful and multiply."

This is the lesson of the parable. "To one he gave five talents, and to another two, and to another one. To everyone according to his proper ability.... He that had received one talent went and digged in the earth and hid his lord's money... 'Lord, I know that you are a hard man. You reap where you have not sown, and gather where you have not strewed, and being afraid I went and hid your talent in the earth. Behold here you have that which is yours.' " [3] The deposit we hold must fructify. We must remember the barren fig-tree.

Holiness is not a passive obedience to the letter of the law. Great saints are great creators. We will be judged according to our fruits.

Holiness is understanding, and understanding is not possible without a co-creative participation in God's work. There is no dispensation from the living act of the spirit which recreates. Intelligence is not at all passive and mirrorlike. The action of love is of vital necessity to understanding. "For to everyone that has shall be given, and he shall abound; but from him that has not, that also which he has shall be taken away." [4]

---

[1] Matth. 10: 26.
[2] Matth. 25: 25.

[3] 1 John 2: 18.
[4] Matth. 25: 25.

Appendices

THE NEO-PLATONISM OF BERGSON

There are two trends in Bergsonism, two interfering systems that sometimes agree and sometimes conflict.

(1) The first is a Realism, an "absolute empiricism," taking its departure from fact scientifically studied for its own sake. This method is explicitly professed by Bergson in the introduction of *La Pensée et le Mouvant* and in his correspondence. "The philosophic method, as I understand it, must be rigorously modeled upon experience (interior or exterior). It does not permit one to express a conclusion that goes the least bit beyond the empirical consideration upon which it rests." [1]

This method, which is very close to Aristotelian and Thomist realism, led Bergson to a criticism of Platonism and to a complete reversal of the orientation of ancient philosophy upon the subjects of time, becoming, the hierarchy of time and eternity, of the real and the possible, of the moving and the immutable, of freedom and necessity. Because of this scientific method, Bergson's philosophy ascends a slope which all ancient thought descends. Bergson psychoanalyzes the unconscious intellectual habits, the latent but tyrannical prejudices of ancient metaphysics that have remained very much alive in modern philosophy. When we were outlining the Hebrew conception of the sensible we noted how helpful Bergson's analyses were in discerning the original attitudes of Hebrew thought in regard to sensible reality, creation and time. Upon these points the affinity between biblical realism and the metaphysical conclusions of Bergsonism gains in significance and value to the extent that Bergson's method was more scientific.

(2) The second aspect of Bergson's thought is, on the contrary, akin to the philosophy of Plotinus and to Neo-Platonism. Al

---

[1] *Lettre au P. de Tonquédec* (*Etudes*, 1912, pp. 514-515).

Bergsonism is molded by a movement which is, in part, the movement of Neo-Platonism: procession, inversion, conversion.

This movement is corrected by Bergson in its first step, thanks to the realist, scientific, empirical method.

The whole originality of Bergson lies in having shown that creation is not a procession in the Neo-Platonic sense of the word: degradation, fall, descent. Bergson is the first philosopher to have understood and reasoned on creation, distinguishing it from fabrication and establishing its positive characteristics against the arguments of Platonism and of the Pantheist systems of Neo-Platonic origin. But Bergson is nonetheless fascinated by the Neo-Platonic tradition and his work is full of the themes that we also find in Plotinus, the Cabala, Spinoza, Hegel and Schelling. We need only read Bergson's course on Plotinus at the Collège de France to discern to what extent he interprets Plotinus as his own doctrine. To explain Plotinus he only needs to draw from his own resources following a certain inclination. The same holds true for Spinoza: "I believe I told you once already that I always feel at home when I re-read the Ethics, and that I am surprised at this since most of my theses seem to be (and are in fact) quite contrary to Spinozism." [1]

Bergson speaks of this movement that he rediscovers in Spinoza: "Spinoza's intuition is an intuition which no formula, no matter how simple, will be simple enough to express. To be content with an approximation let us say that it is the sentiment of a coincidence of the act by which our mind knows truth perfectly, and the operation by which God engenders it. It is the idea that the "conversion" of the Alexandrians, when completed, becomes but one with their "procession;" and that when man, issued from the divinity, succeeds in returning to it, he finally perceives but a single movement in the place of the two contrary movements, departure and return, that he saw before. Here moral experience takes it upon itself to resolve a logical contradiction, and to bring it about, by a sudden suppression of time that the return should be a going." [2]

* * *

Inversion

Inversion is "the creative gesture undoing itself." Inversion is responsible for the materiality of reality, the multiplicity of

[1] *Lettre à Jankélévitch*, in *Evidences*, 1951.
[2] *La Pensée et le Mouvant*, p. 241, P.U.F. 1946.

beings, the "spatialization" of things, the retrospective orientation of our understanding, and for *care* which alienates our thought.

"All these analyses reveal to us an effort within life to ascend the slope which matter descends." [1]

"In the universe itself we must distinguish two opposite movements, one of "descent," the other of "ascent." [2] "The physical... (is) the psychical inverted." [3] "A cosmology that would be an inverted psychology." [4] "It is the same inversion of the same movement which creates both the intellectuality of the mind and the materiality of things." [5]

"At the bottom of 'spirituality' on the one hand and 'materiality' with intellectuality on the other, there would therefore be two processes oppositely directed, and one would pass from the first to the second by way of inversion, perhaps even by mere interruption, if it is true that inversion and interruption are terms that must be considered synonymous here." [6]

"Everything that appears *positive* to the physician and the geometer would become, from this new point of view, an interruption or an inversion of true positiveness which would have to be defined in psychological terms." [7]

Individuation depends on both the positive movement: — "life is a tendency, and the essence of a tendency is to develop itself by ramification" [8] — and the movement of inversion, materiality: "matter effectively divides what was only virtually multiple, and in this sense individuation is in part the work of matter, and in part the result of what life holds in itself." [9] "Matter is primarily that which divides and specifies... matter distinguishes, separates, resolves into individualities, tendencies which before were mingled in the original vital impulse." [10]

Matter is *principium individuationis*, the principle of individuation. Now, if matter is the subsidence of the creative impulse falling back in a rain, we must presume that this scattering, this tendency to multiplicity appeared at the very beginning of the life stream. At the source of reality the tendency to dispersion is at work. Starting

---

[1] *L'Evolution créatrice*, p. 246, P.U.F. 1946.
[2] *L'Evolution créatrice*, p. 11, P.U.F. 1946.
[3] *L'Evolution créatrice*, p. 203, P.U.F. 1946.
[4] *Ibid.*, p. 209.   [5] *Ibid.*, p. 207.
[6] *Ibid.*, p. 202.   [7] *Ibid.*, p. 209.
[8] *Ibid.*, p. 100.   [9] *Ibid.*, p. 259.
[10] *L'Energie spirituelle*, p. 22, P.U.F. 1946.

from the One there is a schism, a separation which causes the materiality of reality and the multiplicity of things. We have here an idea that is very close to that of the Platonic *chōra*. Aristotle identifies Plato's *chōra* with matter.

To Plotinus multiple realities proceed from the One by descending, and by separating themselves as they get farther from their source. To Bergson they spring from this source and "realize" themselves, become "things" when the fountain falls back and undoes itself in exhaustion. Both follow the same pattern but Bergson reverses it by considering creation a positive act. To one as to the other the genesis of the multiple proceeds from an inversion that is rooted in an original schism. This is a theme that haunted the great Cabalistic cosmogonies up to Hegel: at the origin, there is an *Entzweiung*. In German romanticism this separation is blamed upon intelligence. Consciousness would be at fault.

"The name of that Sephira, Bina, can be taken to mean not only "understanding," but also "that which divides things amongst themselves," in other words, differentiation." [1] After the Cabala, philosophers initiated to the Jewish Gnosis and familiar with Plotinus, will pick up this interpretation of the narrative of the fall. Knowledge is the cause of the multiple. This interpretation mingles Manichean Gnostic currents with biblical tradition. When we consider the function of intelligence in Bergsonism we are inclined to find an affinity between certain aspects of his thought and the Gnostic intuitions of the Cabala and of German philosophy.

Since individuation is achieved by a negative process one may wonder whether individuality and, *a fortiori*, personality, are given a consistent metaphysical foundation.

"Generally when one and the same object appears simple on one side and indefinitely complex on the other, the two aspects are far from having the same importance, or rather the same degree of reality." [2]

In this case would not a "converted" mind, with an authentic knowledge of reality, see the multiplicity of individual beings vanish like an illusion peculiar to an inverted, care-ridden and too human understanding? We are very close to Spinoza. "Therefore the current (of Life) passes through human generations, subdividing itself into individuals. This subdivision was already

---

[1] Scholem, *loc. cit.*
[2] BERGSON, *L'Evolution créatrice*, p. 90, P.U.F. 1946.

vaguely traced out in it, but would not have become apparent without matter.   Thus souls are constantly created which nevertheless pre-existed in a certain sense." [1]   One may recall that Spinoza believed in metempsychosis.

So individual existence comes from materiality, from *ensomatosis*.   "When, how, and why do (souls) enter this body which we see, before our eyes, arising quite naturally from a mixed cell taken from the bodies of its two parents?" [2]   Like Plato and Plotinus, Bergson is a dualist.   He always speaks of the body as of a substance distinct from the other substance: soul.   This is his heritage from Plato and Descartes.

To Bergson the body is care.   It is defined in terms of function.   The brain is the organ of attention to life; and organ of action and of action alone.   The body is a servant.   It is there for care.   To become disinterested is to use the body no longer and to pass to the level of pure memory and of mind.   Immortality is Platonic.   One cannot conceive the utility of a body for a being who does not need reality to provide for himself.   The body is the concern of a soul that is preoccupied with the world and has taken the world's matter on itself in order to act upon it.   Its concern has organized a germ according to the requirements of the functions necessary to life.   The eye is the concern of a soul that wishes to see certain aspects of reality which are useful to its bodily existence.   We have not sight for the sake of seeing but sight for the sake of acting.   Care restricts knowledge.   The eye restricts vision to what is useful.   "Sight is a power that should *by rights* reach an infinity of things that are inaccessible to our eyes.   But such a vision would not be prolonged in action; it would be suitable for a ghost, but not for a living being.   The sight of a living being is an efficient sight restricted to objects upon which the being can act: it is a *canalized* sight." [3]

Cf. Plotinus: "It is as though, knowing all about some science, one never considered but a single theorem....   Likewise this soul... we may say, leaps out from the universal being into a particular being upon which it directs a particular activity." [4]

If authentic knowledge is to turn away from care, then one must turn away from the body.   *Sōma sēma,* "the body is a prison."

---

[1] *L'Evolution créatrice*, p. 270, P.U.F. 1946.
[2] *L'Evolution créatrice*, p. 269. P.U.F. 1946.
[3] *L'Evolution créatrice*, p. 94, P.U.F. 1946.
[4] Cf. PLOTINUS, *Enn.* 6: 4, 16.

Inversion is "spatialization" for things, and exteriorization for the mind. Inversion inclines the mind to think about the exterior rather than the interior, because it is not a question of knowing for the sake of knowing, but for the sake of acting.

Now the exterior is what falls to the inferior. The attention given to exterior things, required by our bodily condition, is care and is also inversion. *Inversion and care are the same movement.* Mind becomes a stranger to itself. It knows that which by nature is foreign to itself better than itself. "The (soul) is not allowed to stay within itself because it is constantly drawn towards the outer, inferior and obscure regions." [1]

Mind, in its concern with outer things, leans down to them and therefore looks in a direction counter to the flow of the creative act. Hence the retrospective orientation of our understanding. From this there follow two consequences that are correlative:

(1) Understanding, because it considers matter so to speak in reverse, is incapable of grasping the positive genesis of matter. "Understanding is characterized by a natural incomprehension of life." All that is creation escapes it.

(2) On the other hand it attributes positive reality to negative ideas. Because of its inversion it is inclined to give priority to the negative over the positive, to nothingness over being, to disorder over order, to the possible over the real. Nothingness and disorder would seem to have priority by rights. "Existence appears to me as a conquest over nothingness. I tell myself that there could, and even should, not be anything. I am then surprised to see that something exists." [2] "The idea that there might not be any order at all, and that the mathematical order of things, being a conquest over disorder, possesses a positive reality." [3] It "should be, it seems, by rights." [4]

"We proceed from absence to presence, from void to fulness, as a result of the fundamental illusion of our understanding." [5] "This retrospective vision is... the natural function of our intelligence." [6]

---

[1] PLOTINUS, *Enn.* I: 6, 5, 35.
[2] *L'Evolution créatrice*, p. 276, P.U.F. 1946.
[3] *L'Evolution créatrice*, p. 221, P.U.F. 1946.
[4] *L'Evolution créatrice*, p. 232, P.U.F. 1946.
[5] *L'Evolution créatrice*, p. 275, P.U.F. 1946.
[6] *L'Evolution créatrice*, p. 238, P.U.F. 1946.

All difficulties in metaphysics arise from the fact that we attempt to think of the living real, in its creation, in a positive sense, with an understanding that is inverted because it is care-ridden. Inversion, which is an interruption of the creative drive, is the explanation of the understanding's asthenia, its impotence to think of that which is life and strength.   Care accounts for the constant confusion that the mind makes between creation and fabrication. All the pseudo-concepts and pseudo-problems of metaphysics arise out of this two-fold failing which has a single origin: inversion. This is the cause of the materiality of things and of the "thingyfying" tendency of the mind and of "that invincible inclination that makes us think always of *things* rather than of *advances*." [1]

* * *

Consciousness is *alienated* in materiality, in nature.

"Everything takes place as if a broad current of consciousness has penetrated into matter." [2]

"Nature turns mind away from mind, and turns mind towards matter."

"Our personality is what we should know best.   But it is not at all so; our personality is, as it were, a stranger to itself, whereas matter is familiar to it and in the presence of matter one feels at home." [3]

The genesis of reality is effected by an alienation of the creative consciousness into materiality which is its own inversion.   The mind is in exile, a captive.   This theme shows a certain similarity to the old Gnostic theme that is found very early in Manicheism, and later in the Cabala (the exile of the *Schekkina*, the captive sparks that must be freed), and in Hegel *(Entfremdung)*.

"Consciousness... in order to free itself," [4] Bergson writes, and we see by this that consciousness, to him, is a prisoner.   Consciousness had been alienated in the inferior organisms, in the vegetable and animal kingdoms.   It had been put to sleep, annulled.

---

[1] *La Pensée et le Mouvant*, p. 135, P.U.F. 1946.
[2] *L'Evolution créatrice*, p. 182, P.U.F. 1946.
[3] *La Pensée et le Mouvant*, p. 41, P.U.F. 1946.
[4] *L'Evolution créatrice*, p. 186, P.U.F. 1946.

Throughout the course of evolution it is trying to find itself again. The development of the nervous system and of the processes of cerebration tend towards this goal — toward the liberation of something that had been imprisoned. Only in man does the development reach this goal.

Man, thanks to the structures of his brain, can *detach* himself and find leisure. Man, who can be disinterested in regard of useful action, who frees himself from the hypnotism of the useful, from the servitude of care, approaches freedom and authentic knowledge, With man, conciousness reaches its rest, its sabbath. With man. in the words of Hegel, consciousness becomes a consciousness of self. From the very beginning consciousness tended to contemplation and to freedom. Life is a tendency to contemplation. [1] But it is an imprisoned and exiled contemplation seeking a return, suffering from nostalgia. Man effects this return and this liberation. "With man consciousness breaks the chain.... In man, and in man alone, it frees itself." [2] "Thus, in the last analysis, man would be the motive for the entire organization of life upon this planet." [3]

* * *

Conversion

Conversion is the move by which we reverse the negative movement of inversion and return to the direction of the original creative movement. Conversion rebuilds all that inversion undid.

"Our mind can follow the reverse procedure... It must do violence to itself. It must reverse the direction of the operation by which it habitually thinks; it must invert, or rather continually refashion its categories.... *To philosophize is to reverse the habitual direction of work and of thinking.*" [4] One must reach "experience at its very source, or rather above that decisive *turn* at which, changing course to move in the direction of our utility, it becomes properly human experience." [5]

Inversion was an interruption of the creative drive. Conversion will be a resumption of that creative operation. Inverted understanding is asthenic. Converted thought is co-creative. "For

[1] Cf. PLOTINUS, *Enn.* 3: 8.   [2] *L'Evolution créatrice*, p. 264.
[3] *L'Evolution créatrice*, p. 186. Cf. *Les Deux Sources de la Morale et de la Religion*, p. 271, P.U.F. 1946.
[4] *La Pensée et le Mouvant*, pp. 213-214, P.U.F. 1946.
[5] *Matière et Mémoire*, p. 205, P.U.F. 1946.

our consciousness to coincide with some aspect of its principle it would have to detach itself from what is finished and attach itself to what is *in the making*. Turning back and twisting upon itself, the faculty of *seeing* would have to become but one with the act of *willing*." [1] Converted thought, in other words intuition, accompanies the creative act in its invention. "We know and understand only what we can, to a certain extent, reinvent." [2]

Correlatively, and in the same movement, conversion is to liberate oneself from care and from the servitude of useful human action. "One should *detach* this attention from the practically interesting aspects of the universe and *turn it back* to that which, practically, is useless. This conversion of attention would be philosophy itself." [3] "The difficulties inherent to metaphysics, the antinomies it arouses, the contradictions into which it falls, the division into antagonistic schools, and the irreducible opposition of systems, come, for the most part, from the fact that we apply to disinterested investigation of reality the processes we currently use to a practically useful end." [4] This is a leit-motiv of Bergson's work. Any authentic knowledge is a disinterested knowledge. As with Heidegger, care is responsible for inauthenticity.

Still one should note that the Bergsonian "conversion" is not a "flight" as it is in Platonism or Plotinism. There is no question of leaving sensible reality to escape towards a timeless world. One should, on the contrary, know reality as it is, i. e., essentially *in the process* of creation, in genesis, temporal. We can see how Bergson corrects the Neo-Platonic *"epistrophe"* by integrating it. [5] Conversion introduces the mind to a contemplative knowledge. But this contemplation is not opposed to action as such. It is opposed to care, to preoccupation. For creative action is freedom itself, essentially gratuitous. "Nature appears as an enormous flowering of unforseeable novelty. The force animating it seems to create with love, for no special reason, for pleasure." [6] The artist is the person who sees reality as it is; such as it was created. And "the duty of the philosopher should be to examine the living without any consideration of practical utility, by freeing himself from specifically intellectual habits and forms." [7]

[1] *L'Evolution créatrice*, p. 238, P.U.F. 1946.
[2] *La Pensée et le Mouvant*, p. 95, P.U.F. 1946.
[3] *La Pensée et le Mouvant*, p. 153, P.U.F. 1946.
[4] Intr. à la Met., *La Pensée et le Mouvant*, p. 212, P.U.F. 1946.
[5] Cf. *La Pensée et le Mouvant*, p. 153, P.U.F. 1946.
[6] *L'Energie spirituelle*, p. 24, P.U.F. 1946.
[7] *L'Evolution créatrice*, p. 197, P.U.F. 1946.

Appendix II

CARE

The idea of care is very important in the tradition of Neo-Platonic thought. Care is correlative to *"ensomatosis"* (to being "embodied"). "The steersman of a storm-tossed ship is so intent on saving it that he forgets his own interest and never thinks that he is recurrently in peril of being dragged down with the vessel; similarly the souls are intent upon contriving for their charges and finally come to be pulled down by them. They are fettered in bonds of sorcery, gripped and held by their concern for the realm of nature." [1]

To Bergson also, understanding seems essentially care-ridden because it is enslaved to the needs of bodily existence.

In biblical tradition care has a quite different metaphysical significance. It is not the consequence of bodily existence, of *"ensomatosis;"* it is not a constitutive part of being in the world. In other words, bodily existence is neither fall nor sin.

In Neo-Platonic metaphysics salvation is a "conversion" that frees us both from the alienation of care, and from the fragmentation which bodily existence entails. Asceticism is the principle of salvation.

From the biblical point of view, care is the product of a spiritual attitude. Liberation, "the freedom of the children of God," is possible in this world; the "body" is no hindrance to this. Indeed the glorious life will not be a flight out of the body but resurrection. Liberation from care is not found in *"epistrophē"* but in *"metonoia;"* not in "conversion" but in renewal of the intellect."

---

[1] PLOTINUS, *Enn.* 4: 3, 17, Tr. McKenna.

Thus contemplation has a different meaning within each system. To Neo-Platonism it implies flight, whereas to the Bible it is entirely compatible with action and with work.

* * *

The Sabbath suspends alienation in work. That is its metaphysical significance. "The contemporary age," writes Gabriel Marcel, "— and one might say as much for any age — is characterized, so it seems to me, by what I might call a hypertrophy of the idea of function.... The individual is inclined to appear, in his own eyes and in the eyes of others, as a simple sheaf of functions... vital functions... and social functions; consumer function, producer function, citizen function, etc." [1] It is the purpose of the Sabbath to make a break between man and his functions, and to prevent the "identification of man with these functions." "One hardly need stress the impression of stifling sorrow made upon one by a world thus centered upon function." This sorrow is the sorrow of servitude, which is a death of the spirit. The Sabbath is the beginning of a liberation, a renewal of awareness of man's metaphysical reality, a recognition of his true destiny which is obscured in the flurry of work and of "diversion."

As with all the rest, the New Testament extends the significance of the Sabbath. By becoming interior and spiritual the Sabbath reveals itself as a "non-preoccupation" which is the beginning of the spiritual life. Care is the very contrary of the spirit's life and liberty. Neither action nor bodily life in the world are a servitude. By giving care a different position from that which it had in Neo-Platonism, biblical thought frees action from the Manichean weight that was upon it. In the biblical perspective contemplative life can very well go hand in hand with the creative action that transforms the world. "I do not pray that you should take them out of the world, but that you should keep them from evil."

It is care that prevents the word from growing in man. "He that receives the seed among thorns is he that hears the word, and the cares of this world (hē merimna tou aiōnos) and the deceitfulness of riches stifle the word and it becomes unfruitful." [2]

---

[1] G. MARCEL, *Position et approches concrètes du Mystère Ontologique*, 1949, p. 46.
[2] Matth. 13: 22; Mark 4: 19; Luke 8: 14.

Care overcharges the heart, i.e., understanding. "Take heed to yourselves lest perhaps your hearts be overcharged with surfeiting and drunkenness, and the cares of this life *(merimnais biotikais)*." [1]

"Take no thought for your soul *(mē merimnate tē psuchē)* what you shall eat, or what you shall drink, nor for your body what you shall put on." "Which of you can by worrying add one cubit to the length of his life. Be not therefore solicitous for the morrow *(mē merimnesete eis tēn aurion)*, for the morrow will be solicitous for itself." [2]

St. Paul tells the Corinthians: "I would have you be without care, *(Thelō humas amerimnous)*. He that is unmarried cares for the things that belong to the Lord, how he may please the Lord. But he that is married cares for the things that are of the world, how he may please his wife." [3]   A very close tie binds care with the world.   In the New Testament the two ideas are united.   One should note that a similar relationship binds these two terms in the philosophy of Heidegger.

---

[1] Luke 21: 34.
[3] I Cor. 7: 32.

[2] Matth. 6: 25 et sq.; cf. Luke 12: 22.

HEBREW THOUGHT AND THE CHURCH

The Church is an organic reality, a *body*.

In nature, all created beings are organic. Mechanical realities are characteristic of human fabrication, "works of human hands." All reality that is not of man's making, all living reality, is organic. The Church is not an organism of the biological order. It is an organism of the *spiritual* order. The cells from which it is made are not only individuals, but conscious and free *persons*. If they belong to the Mystical Body, it is not through biological necessity but through a spiritual choice.

Yet the Church is an organism in the most realistic sense of the word. The ties are not visible that bind together the cells of this body, but because they are imperishable they are more real than those of sensible bodies. All the persons who are integrated, incorporated in the Mystical Body are bound together by a *vinculum substantiale* which quickens them as it unites them. This substantial bond is the Holy Ghost, the real presence of God's *Memra,* the inhabitation of the Anointed.

The Church, like any organism, exists only because it is one. To be, and to be one, are synonymous for the Church. No cell belonging to a body could subsist out of this body. The same thing is true, even more true, in another, spiritual order, of the cells that constitute Mystical Body.

* * *

The Church was *born.*

In this it only conforms itself, on its own level, to the universal law of birth. "Within a universe in a state of evolution, one may say that the fundamental structural law (the only law in a certain sense) is that EVERYTHING IS BORN, in other words, that everything appears in relation to an antecedent." [1]

The Church was born of Christ. It was born in blood, in the blood of the Lord and in the blood of the martyrs.

But this birth was prepared for. In a sense the Church was born with Abraham, when he left Ur in Chaldea and went forth not knowing where he was going. Throughout the Old Testament Israel is spoken of as Someone, a Betrothed, a Spouse: "I have loved you with an everlasting love, O virgin of Israel." [2] "Thus says the Lord to Jerusalem: your root and your birth is of the land of Canaan, your father was an Amorrhite, and your mother a Cephite, and when you were born, in the day of your birth your cord was not cut, neither were you washed with water for your health, nor salted with salt, nor swaddled with clouts. No eye had pity on you to do any of these things for you out of compassion to you: but you were cast out upon the face of the earth in the abjection of your soul in the day that you were born. And passing by you I saw that you were trodden underfoot in your own blood: and I said to you when you were in your blood: live. I have said to you: live in your blood. I caused you to multiply as the grass of the field: and you increased and grew great, and acquired a perfect beauty: your breasts were fashioned and you attained puberty: but you were naked, utterly naked. And I passed by you, and saw you: and behold your time was come, the time of lovers: and I spread my garment over you and covered your ignominy. And I swore to you and I entered into a covenant with you, says the Lord God: and you became mine." [3]

As with every birth, this birth of the Church came from infinitesimal beginnings.

The salvation which God freely gives to the world is not given ready made. It does not fall on the earth from without like a meteorite. God bids it to be born to grow from within. This means that He demands man's cooperation, for without it this salvation would not be the salvation of man.

Small beginnings are required by the universal law of birth. Two thousand years ago these were a handful of Galileans; four thousand years ago, a tribe, one man, Abraham; a nation, "the

---

[1] P. TEILHARD DE CHARDIN, *La structure phylétique du groupe humain,* in *Annales de Paléontologie,* 1951.

[2] Jer. 31: 3.   [3] Ez. 16.

smallest of all the nations." [1] The principle of this salvation, God's *Memra* (whom John's Gospel calls the Logos), the Prophets call the germ, *Zemach*. Incarnation is brought about by a birth, in littleness and poverty. The Kingdom of God in the Gospels is compared to a grain, the smallest of all seeds. Like every birth, the birth of the Word goes unnoticed at first. To those that were his neighbors this is a stumbling block: "We know his brothers, his mother; how is it possible...?"

* * *

The Church *grows*.

It increases in space and in number by the assimilation of new elements. It grows like a tree. "The Kingdom of Heaven is like a grain of mustard seed which a man took and sowed in his field. It is the least of all seeds but when it is grown up it is greater than all herbs and becomes a tree so that the birds of the air come and dwell in the branches of it." [2]

But the Church's development is not only organic, spatial, quantitative. It is a spiritual development too. The Church's organic growth is accompanied by a progressive explicitation of revelation, by a progress in the understanding of the seed, its foundation, by a theological growth. Revealed truth is not a dead thing. "I shall not leave you orphans: I shall come back to you... the paraclete (interpreter), the Holy Spirit whom my Father will send in my name, he will teach you everything and remind you of everything that I have told you." [3]

To deny the development of the Church, to deny that theology grows organically, that the Church unfolds truths that are, in a sense, new even though they are already present in the seed, is to deny that the Church is a living body.

There is such a thing as infantile nostalgia for the primitive, for the undefined. There are those who regret that the primitive style should have developed and become explicitated; that there is now a technical theology wielding metaphysical arms. Periodically someone attempts the old venture over again: a return to the undefined, to the "primitive" Church. As though the developed tree were less faithful to itself than the seed, as though fidelity consisted in remaining a seed and not growing; as though not to

---

[1] Deut. 7: 7.   [2] Matth. 13: 31-32.
[3] John 14.

develop and not to express itself were the seed's fidelity and life; as though growth were a self-betrayal. The seed is new, young and frail. The tree is complex, covered with rough bark, (and often with scars), but the tree is just as alive as was the seed, and stronger. What is this fear of metaphysical thought? What is this fear of conceptualization? In these fears there is a desire of regression; it is one of the infantile diseases that will remain a permanent temptation for the Church. Newman who made an admirable analysis of this idea of development, writes: "One cause of corruption in religion is the refusal to follow the course of doctrine as it moves on, and an obstinacy in the notions of the past." [1] There is a link between this attitude and that trait of individual psychology, so familiar to analysts, which is called a nostalgia for infancy.

This attempt of regression misunderstands the organic and personal character of the Church and the creative nature of time.

* * *

The Church *assimilates*. From every point of view, metaphysical, sociological, ethnical, etc., the Church, throughout 2000 years, has assimilated a great number of elements taken from the Gentiles. When we say that it assimilates we mean that it takes in and incorporates foreign elements and later evacuates whatever it cannot receive without harm to its integrity. Assimilation is not a passive reception of elements from without. It is a choice, and a transformation of the elements taken in, that actually makes them a part of the organism. In this sense Etienne Gilson has shown how Thomism, in its own synthesis, transformed and gave a new meaning to the Aristotelian elements. This is characteristic of the development of all Christian theology.

The Church has been blamed for assimilating Greek philosophy. Yet to deny the Church this power to assimilate the riches of pagan thought is once again to deny that it is a living body. Any organism grows by assimilation and elimination. Any attempt to restrict oneself purely and simply to the Bible is from the very start impossible and sterile; one would have to start by eliminating whatever is of Greek origin, and then whatever is of Iranian origin, and then whatever is of Babylonian origin, etc. One should under-

---

[1] NEWMAN, *Essay on the Development of Christian doctrine*, Chap. V, Sec. I: 8.

stand instead that incarnation is a birth and a growth that finds its nourishment in the environment.

Catholic theology, against all comers, and against all the intellectual temptations of the surrounding philosophical atmosphere, has preserved the great ideas of biblical metaphysics: the excellence of visible reality, the necessary mediation of this sensible reality in the economy of our salvation, the Real Presence in the Church, in the consecrated elements, in the eucharistic bread and wine, the mediation of concrete historical reality. Catholic theology has held on to biblical realism; in the definitions of the Councils she carefully, jealously marked off the doctrinal points that could not be abandoned without losing all the essence of biblical theology. In this way, Catholic theology *continues* the metaphysical tradition of the Bible, just as Catholic liturgy continues the biblical poetics of the elements, the poetics of fire, water, salt, etc. We have a world which is poetic-throughout because it is significant-throughout. Poetry is no more the sole property of the magicians of language; poetry is henceforth the life of any man who lives in a universe where elements are words.

Catholic theology has been faithful to the vital demands of biblical metaphysics in spite of the philosophical environment of the western world in which it grew. While many believed that Greek philosophy, and particularly the philosophy of Aristotle, was identical with Reason itself, the Church has always rejected the temptation to Fideism by maintaining that faith is an understanding.

By supporting and maintaining the reality of God's presence and the spiritual theology of faith, Catholic theology demonstrated its independence of the civilizations within which it developed, and the supernatural assistance that assures the autonomy of this development.

The paradox (to western minds) of these dogmas has allowed the Church to achieve that other paradox which is holiness. There must be real presence if there are to be saints. Without the reality of God's presence, without the mediation of consecrated, sensible reality, without the mediation of the historical Fact and of the sacred History, one may very well become a moral man, a virtuous man, but one cannot become a saint. Carnal realities are indispensable, in order to reach the spiritual reality which is supernatural. The abstract and the disincarnate do not lead to the supernatural order of holiness. We have said before that the Gnostic illusion was to have confused the abstract and the spiritual. To biblical and Christian realism, on the contrary, holiness is not an evasion. It demands instead the mediation of concrete reality, of the neighbor, of the historical. Moral idealism stands at the antipodes of Christianity.

Printed in Belgium by DESCLÉE & Cie, ÉDITEURS, S. A. Tournai. — 10.391